S0-BJL-945

Moline Public Library
3210 41st Street
Moline IL 61265

APR   2012

Learn to Spin

with ANNE FIELD

3 0067 00004 3706

Learn to Spin

with ANNE FIELD

SPINNING BASICS

T
TRAFALGAR SQUARE
North Pomfret, Vermont

First published in the United States of America in 2011 by
Trafalgar Square Books, North Pomfret, Vermont 05053

Printed in China

Published in 2011 by David Bateman Ltd, Auckland, New Zealand

Text © Anne Field, 2011
Typographical design © David Bateman Ltd, 2011

All rights reserved. Except for the purpose of fair review, no part may be stored or
transmitted in any form or by any means, electronic or mechanical, including recording
or storage in any information retrieval systems, without permission in writing from the
publisher. No reproduction may be made, whether by photocopying or by any other
means, unless a license has been obtained from the publisher or its agent.

ISBN 978-1-57076-492-9
Library of Congress Control Number: 2011929194

Book design: Alice Bell

Photographic credits:
Cover: author photograph Mark Field; all others Tony Clark
Ashford Handicrafts Ltd (Tina Gill) pp. 17–20, 22 (bottom), 23, 37–40, 43–48; John Hunter
    pp. 77, 78, 98, 113, 114, 147, 183, 185; iStock pp. 117 (top right), 129 (left), 141 (top), 148, 149,
    165, 169, 177. All others by Tony Clark, unless credited otherwise.
Drawings: Mike Wakelin

Acknowledgements

It is hard to know where to begin thanking people who have helped me with this book. In my 50 years of spinning I have learnt so much from hundreds of spinners, wheel manufacturers and suppliers of fibre. Throughout the book I have named those who have worked with me on it as it is important they get the credit. I am deeply grateful to all these new and old friends.

Without the following support, this book could not have been written:
- to all the spinners who have generously spun, knitted and crocheted the samples and projects in this book; their amazing skills will now reach a wider audience.
- to Ashford Handicrafts Ltd who kindly loaned me much of the equipment used in the photographs and the use of their photographer, Tina Gill.

Photographs are a very important part of a book like this, as they explain techniques more clearly than words can. My heartfelt thanks to my team of photographers:
- to Tony Clark, my son-in-law, whose patience and skills made the technical photographs so clear and easy to follow.
- to Tina Gill, from Ashfords, who took all the equipment shots.
- to John Hunter, for the model shots.

I had the best of fleeces, fibres and advice from the suppliers who are such a credit to the craft of spinning. Many thanks to them for providing me with such excellent raw materials to work with. Thanks also to Mike Wakelin for his detailed drawings. I have learnt so much in writing this book and it is thanks to all the above.

Anne Field

Contents

INTRODUCTION   **11**

PART ONE: LEARNING TO SPIN   **13**

1: THE SPINNING PROCESS   **15**

Getting started; What type of wheel should you start with?;
Basic spinning techniques; Spinning; Plying; Skeining; Washing;
Calculating the amount of yarn needed for each project
Projects: Knitted scarf; Woven runner

2: WHEELS & HOW THEY WORK   **37**

Drive ratio; Measuring yarn size; Electronic spinning wheels;
Wheel maintenance; Which wheel is best for you

3: OTHER WAYS TO SPIN   **51**

Worsted spinning; Semi-worsted spinning; Woollen yarn;
Semi-woollen spinning; Spinning from the fold; Spindle spinning; Conclusion
Projects: Embroidered cross-stitch; Woven worsted-spun fabric; Woollen hat;
Feather & fan shawl/scarf

PART TWO: ANIMAL FIBRES   **81**

4: WOOL   **85**

Wool basics; Sheep breeds; Black & coloured sheep;
Sorting a fleece; Choosing a fleece; Washing a fleece
Project: Jacket

5: ALPACA   **101**

Shearing; Skirting; Washing a fleece; Huacaya; Suri; Plying; Washing
the yarn; Uses; Changing the characteristics
Projects: Woven beaded alpaca scarf; Crocheted hoodie

Contents

6: SILK   117
Spinning; Plying; Washing; Uses; Changing the characteristics
Projects: Knitted silk scarf; Woven silk scarves

7: MOHAIR   129
Shearing; Skirting; Washing a fleece; Spinning a yarn to match the characteristics;
Preparation; Changing the characteristics
Projects: Knitted socks; Woven mohair scarf; Mohair squares

8: ANGORA RABBIT   141
Preparation; Spinning; Uses
Projects: Booties; Scarf

■ **PART THREE: PLANT & MANUFACTURED FIBRES**   149
9: COTTON   153
Spinning a yarn to match the characteristics; Preparation; Spinning;
Plying; Washing; Uses
Projects: Child's beret; Small cardigan

10: MANUFACTURED FIBRES   165
Cellulose fibres; Regenerated protein fibres; Synthetic fibres

■ **PART FOUR: MIXING & MATCHING FIBRES**   171
11: BLENDED FIBRES   175
Commercially prepared fibre; Blending your own fibres;
Plying two different yarns together; Brushing the finished garment
Projects: Scarf; Spinning-wheel shawl; Child's beanie

12: NOVELTY YARNS   189
Spinning lumpy, bumpy yarn on purpose;
Spiral yarn; Bouclé yarn; Knot yarn; Navajo plying;
Adding beads to yarn; Felted yarn

GLOSSARY   197

FURTHER READING   198

INDEX   201

Introduction

NEARLY 50 YEARS ago I saw my first spinning wheels. I had done some weaving but had no thought for the yarn I was using to weave with, or any idea of how yarn was made. Threads had always been there; in weaving, sewing and knitting. Yarn was ready-made, bought in shops, waiting to be made into something useful. It seemed such a leap to me that I could go one step back and make my own yarn.

It looked such a relaxing process too, as I watched my two neighbours sitting outside on a sunny spring day under the apple trees spinning. And it looked easy! We had just moved into a flat next door. I asked if they could teach me to spin and was loaned a wheel. In those days, 1961 in New Zealand, there were probably about 10 spinners and I was lucky enough to have two of them as my neighbours. There had been many groups of spinners during the Second World War, spinning on Ashford wheels and knitting wool for the soldiers overseas as wool was hard to come by, but only one group continued to spin. I asked one of those wartime spinners why she didn't continue spinning after the war, but she said it was a 'war effort' not a relaxing hobby.

I often wonder what would have happened in my life if we had not chosen that particular flat to live in. The reason for choosing that apartment was the loom I saw in the corner of our future landlady's room when we were being interviewed. I did not know at the time but my landlady was Ida Lough, an international tapestry weaver. She was my mentor for many years and influenced me greatly, as from the beginning I viewed weaving and spinning as something that could be more than a pleasurable hobby.

Soon my husband made me a spinning wheel out of an iron Singer sewing machine wheel which I used until we could afford a 'proper' wheel. It took me a year to save the £35 for a Bartlett wheel. It was a large Saxony wheel and it served me well for many years. But that first wheel saw me through my struggles to produce some usable yarn. I only had raw fleece with no way of preparing it, but luckily New Zealand fleece has always been long-stapled and clean. I can still remember the frustration of trying to push thick, lumpy, over-twisted yarn through the orifice. And I was not told that you ply going backwards! But eventually the magic moment arrived when my feet and my hands worked in unison, not in conflict.

What I needed then was this book. There was nothing I could find written about spinning so everything I wanted to know I found out for myself. This has probably made me a better teacher and writer and I hope this book will put my 50 years of finding things out for myself, or from other spinners, to good use. Teaching and writing about spinning and weaving has given me a worldwide group of friends and a meditative pastime which has soothed my soul. It has led me to many parts of the world, meeting interesting and dedicated manufacturers of wheels and looms. It has given me an income, pushed me into getting a university degree, and changed my life.

Spinning has changed as well. Fifty years ago we usually spun with wool. Now we can spin many other fibres: alpaca, mohair, silk, cotton, angora, flax and many other cellulose fibres such as Tencel and bamboo and we can blend these fibres together. We have a vast array of spinning wheels to chose from, and many tools for preparing the fibres. So begin this journey with me to explore the wonderful world of spinning.

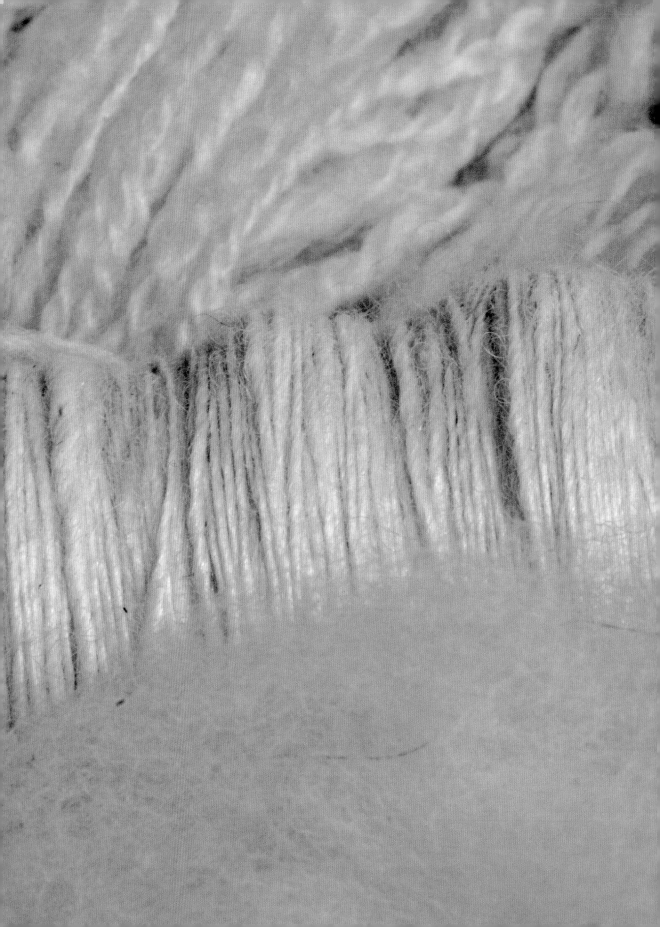

Part One
LEARNING TO SPIN

I Learning to spin

IN THIS FIRST section we begin with the basic spinning process which will provide you with enough information on materials and wheels to get you started on this voyage of discovery. To begin with, you will be happy to spin a yarn and experience the excitement of just making a continuous thread.

However, there comes a time when just making a thread — any thread — is not enough. You will soon want to spin different types and sizes of yarn. Once the basics are grasped, it is time to introduce you to the wide variety of spinning techniques, allowing you to spin yarns suitable for finished projects. You will learn how to control the process and about different yarn structures.

To give you this control, an understanding of how wheels work is a necessary part of the process. Spinning wheels are not only beautiful things in themselves; they are also functional and complex machines that have evolved over hundreds of years. There are many types of wheels and in this section we will look at how they function and what would be the best wheel for you.

In my workshops I ask each student what they do with their finished yarn. Some spin wool fine enough to knit shawls that will pass through a wedding ring. Some spin to weave thick floor rugs. I have also been told by several students that they just pat their wool, or hang it on the wall to admire it. If you want to do more than just look at your beautiful skeins, there are projects in this section of the book which I hope will inspire you to use your spun yarn in different ways.

My best advice to you is to go for it!

The spinning process

▇ GETTING STARTED

IT IS EASIEST to start your spinning experience with wool because this is the most common fibre used for spinning. But first you need to know something about this fibre. In Chapter 4 we will go into more detail, but a brief description will do to get you started.

Wool comes from sheep and there are many different breeds, each of which has its own characteristics. I started with Romney wool because it is the most common New Zealand sheep and has a staple length of about 10–15cm (4–6in), which makes it easy to spin. A staple is a bundle of wool fibres within a fleece; these separate staples allow air movement within a fleece and keep the sheep warm and dry. Another name for a staple is a lock. Romney sheep produce a medium fibre, suitable for outdoor garments and hard-wearing enough that one jersey could be handed down and outlast my three children — no mean feat.

Each wool fibre is covered in minute, overlapping scales (see page 86) which help with the drafting (the pulling out) of the fibres as each fibre seems to pull out adjacent fibres and they do not slip as easily as some other fibres such as silk. Wool is greasy and it is this grease which protects the fibres from the weather. Some spinners like the feel and smell of greasy wool, others need to wash the fleece before working on it. In our first home I stored fleeces under our bed and after a while we didn't even notice the smell. However, it was a small flat and visitors did sometimes comment unfavourably.

The crimp (the wave pattern) in each staple gives wool its elasticity and it is this characteristic which makes wool so suitable for comfortable clothing. The finer the wool, the more crimp, but even very coarse wools with little or no crimp, such as Drysdale, can be used as carpet wool. As you progress with your spinning you will learn about the many breeds of sheep and will soon have your favourites. Some spinners love the finer breeds, which they spin into fine yarn for shawls; others like to spin thick yarns for floor rugs. The variety of yarns you can spin is endless.

With a very clean, open fleece, you can spin straight from the fleece as I did when I first began. Of course I had no choice because that was all that was available. Now we can buy fleece that has been commercially prepared for spinners. This is wool that has been prepared by drawing the washed fleece through a series of metal teeth to open it up. In industry the wool goes through several large rollers, which open and card the wool into a batt (the full width of the carders) or sliver (a thinned-out portion of the batt). Roving and tops

1.1 Romney sheep (top) and fleece.

are the product of a further combing process which aligns the fibres so they lie in a parallel formation.

We can use hand and drum carders to make batts/slivers, or use wool combs and flick carders to make rovings and tops. There are many small manufacturers who card wool just for spinners and your local spinning-wheel supplier will generally have some for sale. Later I will explain how to card your own wool but for now we will use this commercially prepared wool. As it has been prepared for you, it means a quick start with no wastage.

When using unwashed fleece, always wash your hands carefully after you have handled or spun the fleece. You never know where the sheep has been!

Spinning is simply the action of drafting the fibres and then putting a twist in them. The amount you draft determines the size of the yarn and the twist gives the needed strength. Try this for yourself.

YOU WILL NEED:
Some carded wool or a staple or two from a clean, open fleece
This is a slow way to make yarn. There are two ways of speeding up the process as both these pieces of equipment let you draft and twist at the same time.

1.2 From left: fleece wool, hand-carded fleece and coloured top.

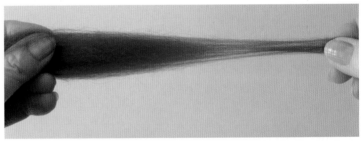

1.3 Take a staple of fleece or a 15cm (6in) length of carded fleece. Grasp each end of the fibre and draft it so it thins out. You will feel the fibres moving past each other.

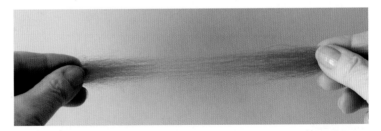

1.4 The fibres soon break as they have no strength.

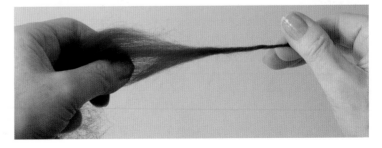

1.5 Draft out another portion of the fibre, at the same time twisting it. This fibre will not break, as the twisting strengthens the fibres and prevents further movement. Now you have yarn.

A spindle

A spindle is a shaft with a whorl, similar to a top. The whorl is usually a circular piece of wood which adds weight and momentum to the shaft. With a spindle, you twirl the shaft with one hand, which adds twist to the fibre, then you draft the attached fibre until the whorl slows down.

A spinning wheel

A spinning wheel has a spindle supported and turned on its side. With the earliest spinning wheels, the spindle was connected by a band to a wheel which was turned by hand. A great wheel and a charkha wheel are of this type. The next innovation was that a treadle was connected to the wheel and feet could be used to turn the wheel instead of fingers. The whorl now has a groove in it to contain the band and it becomes a pulley, although it is usually still called a

1.6 Spindle.

1.7 Spinning wheel. Ashford Traditional: detail of flyer with spindle overlay (A).

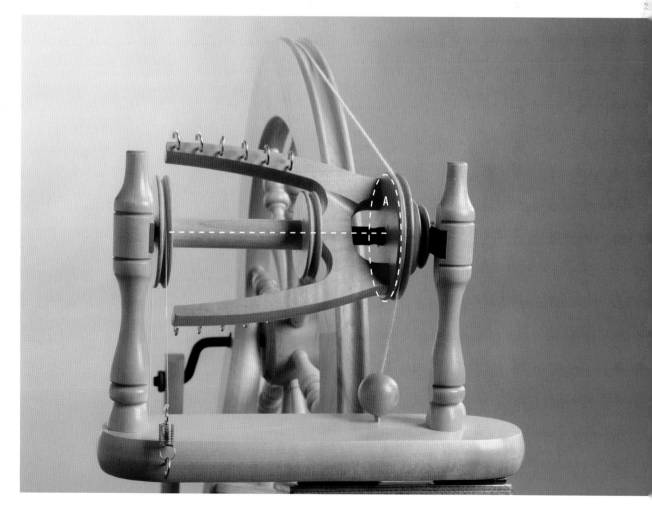

1.8 Great wheel.

1.9 Charkha wheel.

spindle whorl. Thus both hands are free to do the drafting and the process becomes much quicker.

Spindles, great wheels and charkha wheels are still in use today, but the treadle wheel is most commonly used in spinning so we will start with this.

With a spindle, the great wheel and the charkha, the process of twisting the fibres, then winding them around the spindle shaft is two separate actions. On a spinning wheel, the spindle shaft and the yarn holder have separated and become a metal shaft holding a removable bobbin. By making the bobbin revolve at a different speed to the spindle shaft, the yarn is pulled onto the bobbin during the treadling action.

1.10 Ashford Traditional with named parts. Flyer-led wheel with Scotch tension. A) drive wheel; B) drive band; C) spindle whorl; D) bobbin; E) maidens; F) flyer; G) drive band tension knob; H) brake band tension knob; I) treadle; J) footman; K) crankshaft.

■ WHAT TYPE OF WHEEL SHOULD YOU START WITH?

This is a difficult question for a beginner spinner because you do not know what type of yarn you will enjoy spinning the most. It could be fine yarn for shawls or thick yarn for floor rugs. A wheel that has different sizes of whorls (perhaps with a drive ratio of 5–10) is a good buy because you can then spin different sizes of yarn. At this stage you won't know what drive ratio is (see page 38) but when you buy or borrow a wheel ask if the wheel is in this range.

Before you buy a wheel, try a few out. Spinning groups or guilds may have some wheels you could have a play with. Try treadling a few to see which you like. Most shops that sell spinning wheels will also let you have a try. If you have a spinning friend you can take with you, so much the better. If you can get to classes, you should be able to see and try out a variety of wheels, and may be able to borrow a wheel for a few weeks.

Buying a second-hand wheel

These wheels will cost you less but there are some pitfalls to be wary of:

• Check that the drive wheel is not warped. Get someone to stand to the side and watch while you treadle. This is one fault that cannot be fixed.

• Buy a wheel that is a well-known brand as then parts are easy to come by. Some home-made wheels look fine but simply do not work. My mother bought a pretty little wheel from an antique shop. Everything revolved, and she could treadle it, but the bobbin and the flyer went around at the same speed, the yarn would not pull on, and it was useless. It looked good as part of a dried flower arrangement in her hall for years.

• A wheel that hasn't been used for some time may need oiling to make it run smoothly.

• Make sure all the bobbins fit onto the spindle shaft. Again the shaft may need some oil.

• To make sure the wheel revolves easily, treadle as fast as you can, then quickly lift your foot/feet off the treadle. The wheel should continue revolving on its own for about 30 seconds. This proves that all the parts are running smoothly and there is no friction.

If you need a small, lighter wheel, choose an upright wheel (see photo 2.11, page 47) or a folding wheel (see photo 1.11) as these take up less room and are easily carried around. When I lived in Sydney, I took a portable wheel in its bag on the subway to spinning days as it was light to carry. I could put the bag over my shoulder as long as I remembered not to turn around quickly and bump into people. And it could be transported in my car on the front seat with the seat belt holding it in place. With these smaller wheels, you do have to treadle faster so your legs do more work.

If size is not a consideration, a Saxony-type wheel (see page 46) may be your preference. These have the large wheel, the drive wheel, to the side of the flyer and this wheel is usually bigger than the upright wheels where the drive wheel is underneath the flyer. The bigger the wheel, the less work your feet will have to do. There are also electronic wheels where your feet do no work at all (see page 45).

You will need a minimum of three bobbins, the more the better. You will also need a lazy kate, which holds the spare bobbins and is used when plying two or more strands of yarn together, and a niddy noddy, which makes skeins (see page 30). I get so used to these names that I forget how odd sounding they are to non-spinners.

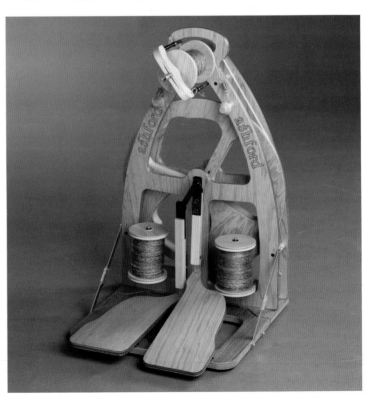

1.11 Joy wheel.

BASIC SPINNING TECHNIQUES

In Chapter 2 we will discuss wheels in much more detail, but I know you are impatient to begin spinning. We will begin with learning to spin on a wheel. Spindle spinning will be covered in Chapter 3. Many spinning teachers start their students on a spindle but, as there were no spindles available when I first began to spin, I went straight onto a wheel. And I still teach beginners this way. Old habits die hard.

TREADLING

Begin by sitting at your wheel and practise treadling. Some spinners prefer the double treadle, where each foot pushes the treadles alternately; others prefer the single treadle. If you can try both types of treadles, and most shops that sell spinning wheels will encourage you to sit and try out both types, see which is easiest. You need a comfortable chair that supports your thighs and back and is the right height. Your shoulders should be relaxed.

Sit so your back rests against the back of the chair and practise treadling with the drive wheel turning in a clockwise direction. Treadle slowly and evenly with an even beat. Think of your heartbeat, as this is a natural rhythm which will make the treadling and spinning process soothing.

Keep your foot (or feet) directly over the treadle so you are pushing down rather away from you. If the wheel is too far away, you will be pushing it away from you, which is a real nuisance. Sometimes on a slippery floor this happens anyway, but a non-slip mat under the wheel will prevent this.

Some wheels use a heel and toe pressure, some just the toe, and others use the whole foot. At spinning days, you will find many spinners spin in their stocking feet as they find this more comfortable. If they do, take a look at their socks. Some of them will be works of art.

TENSION

Some wheels have the drive wheel connected via the band to the bobbin (bobbin-led wheel), and others have the drive wheel connected to the flyer (flyer-led wheel).

You can quickly determine which you have on your wheel by turning the drive wheel slowly by hand. If it is a flyer-led wheel, the flyer will revolve. If it is a bobbin-led wheel, the bobbin will revolve. The flyer is a U-shaped piece of wood or metal on a metal shaft. The flyer arms have hooks to guide the yarn. There is also the double-drive wheel where the doubled drive band is connected to both the bobbin and the flyer.

1.12 Treadling.

1.13 Correct sitting position.

1.14 Tying a leader onto the bobbin.

With all three types of wheel, the bobbin and the flyer must revolve at different speeds to pull the spun yarn onto the bobbin. They each do this in a different way. Setting the tension is how the relevant take-up is adjusted.

Tie a leader, a woollen yarn about 2m (2yds) long, around the centre of the bobbin on your wheel.

Tie the leader tightly onto the bobbin, leaving a long enough tail to go around the bobbin once more, then knot the two ends together. There should be no slippage at all; it is infuriating when the spun yarn won't wind around the bobbin because the knot is too loose. Usually you don't notice this for a while and can't understand why nothing is happening.

Take the long end over the hooks and, using the threading hook, thread it through the orifice, the hollowed-out end of the spindle shaft. Some wheels have a movable hook on the flyer arm instead of several hooks.

Adjusting the tension on a flyer-led wheel (Scotch tension)

With this system the bobbin is slowed down by a brake band which goes across the top of the bobbin and can be tightened or loosened by turning a peg.

This is probably the most common system as there is a wide range of movement when tightening or loosening the brake band and this helps pull on your first lumpy, bumpy yarn. The drive band should be firm but not tightly stretched around the drive wheel and the flyer. It can be adjusted by moving the mother-of-all (see photo 1.17) further away from the drive wheel. The brake band should have no slack in it but will have some give because one end is attached to a spring.

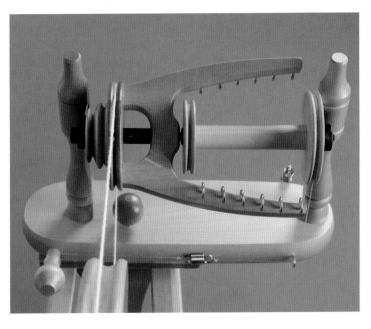

1.15 Ashford Traditional: Scotch tension system.

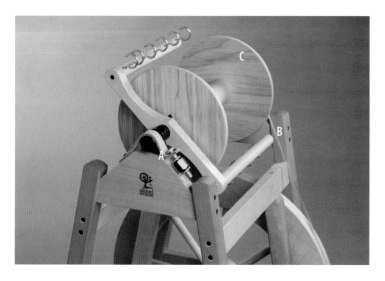

1.16 Country spinning wheel: Irish tension. A) brake band; B) nylon drive band; C) large bobbin.

Adjusting the tension on a bobbin-led wheel (Irish tension)

With this system, the brake band goes around the flyer to slow it down. This system is most often found on wheels which are used for spinning thick yarn and is less common than the Scotch tension or double-drive wheels. The bobbins are usually bigger to hold the thicker yarn. Again the tension is adjusted by tightening or loosening the brake band.

Adjusting the tension on a double-drive wheel

This system has a doubled drive band. It is one continuous band, crossing over so one portion goes around the bobbin and the other around the flyer. To allow for the different speeds of the bobbin and flyer, the whorls are smaller on the bobbin than on the flyer.

1.17 Elizabeth wheel: Double-drive system. A) maidens; B) mother-of-all; C) screw; D) stock; E) smaller whorl; F) larger whorl; G) doubled drive bands.

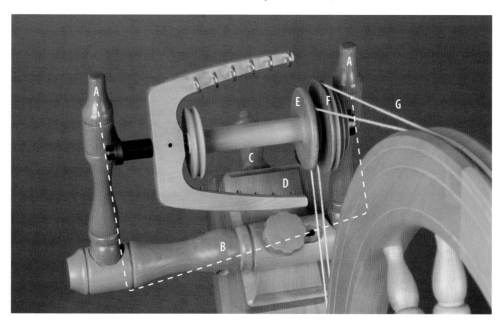

Problem solving

- The leader won't pull on at all.
  Solution: This means the brake band is too loose, so tighten it a fraction at a time until the leader begins to move.
- The leader disappears as soon as you begin to treadle.
  Solution: The brake band is too tight, so loosen it gradually.
- The treadling is hard work.
  Solution: You may have the drive band too tight. Loosen it a little at a time.
- The drive wheel either stops occasionally or goes backwards.
  Solution: You are not treadling consistently and may need more practice.

This means the bobbin revolves faster than the flyer. To adjust the tension, the complete mother-of-all is moved away (or towards) the drive wheel. Moving it away tightens the drive band and the yarn is pulled on faster. Moving it towards the drive wheel slackens the drive band and there is less pull on the yarn. The mother-of-all fits into the base, at the end of which is a handle connected to a screw which engages the mother-of-all. It is interesting that these named parts are feminine, as is the term 'maidens'. The maidens are the uprights that hold the flyer.

Many wheels have provision for both the Scotch and the double-drive system on one wheel. As a beginner you will probably find the Scotch-tension system easier to use until your yarn becomes more consistent, as there is a wider range of adjustment. This allows for a bigger difference between the bobbin and flyer speed and your uneven yarn can be pulled on.

Now you know how the various systems work, we can adjust the tension on the leader on your wheel so you are ready to begin spinning.

Begin treadling with the wheel turning to the right (clockwise). Hold the leader loosely in the fingers of one hand. The full length of the leader hanging from the orifice will begin to move through the hooks onto the bobbin.

If the tension on the brake band is enough, the leader will smoothly pull onto the bobbin. You will be very lucky to have the brake band tension correct on your first attempt.

▋ SPINNING

Use commercially prepared fibre for this, your first lesson in spinning.

1.18 Wind the leader onto the bobbin until about 30cm (12in) is hanging from the orifice. Take a length of fibre about 15cm (6in) in your right hand (back hand), and with your left (front hand) fluff one end up a little and hold the fluffy ends against the leader with the thumb and forefinger. The leader and the fibre should overlap about 5cm (2in) and be pinched together. I am right-handed but I use the left hand for drafting. However, this does not work for everyone. I will call the hand holding the fibre the back hand and the drafting hand the front hand. Try exchanging hands to see which suits you best. Try to rest both hands on your lap while spinning as this is less tiring than holding them above your lap.

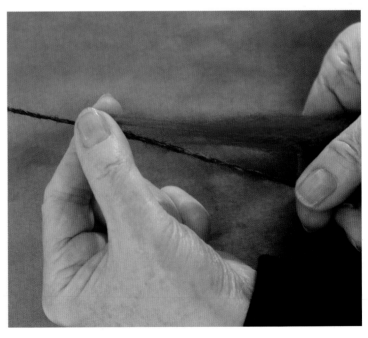

1.19 Begin treadling in a clockwise direction and watch the twist travel down the leader and catch onto the fibre.

1.20 As soon as the fibres have caught onto the leader, move the front hand, still pinching the fibre, towards the orifice, taking with it some of the fibre from the back hand. The back hand holds the fibre just firmly enough to let the wool glide through.

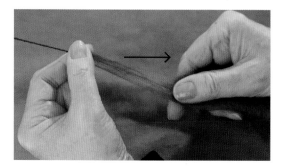

1.21 When your hands are about 5–8cm (2–3in) apart, loosen the pinch of the front hand and slide it back, allowing the twist to follow just in front of the forefinger and thumb holding the fibre. Do not let the twist past this front hand.

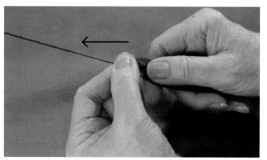

1.22 When the front hand is about 2.5cm (1in) away from the back hand, pinch again and move the front hand forward.

SHORT FORWARD DRAFT

Repeat these movements until the fibre supply in your back hand is used up. The most important point with this spinning method is to never let the twist into the drafting area. You will know when you have got it right when you can see the wool fanning out behind the front hand.

This method of spinning is called the short forward draft. I am not sure whether I spin this way because, all those years ago, this was how I was taught. I think the reason I use my right hand as the back hand that holds the fibre is because I first learnt to spin with unprepared fleece wool. This meant that my strongest hand, my right, was used for aligning the wool staples ready for drafting. Therefore my drafting hand, the left, did less work.

Some spinners prefer to spin by drafting back with the drafting hand rather than drafting forward as I have described here.

This is called the short backward draft. I call myself a 'pusher' as I push the yarn onto the bobbin with my drafting hand. A 'puller' drafts by pulling the fibre back towards the body before letting it move onto the bobbin. Try both methods to see which is easier for you.

25

Problem solving

- The most common mistake is to let the twist get past the front hand and into the drafting area. Once the fibre is twisted, it won't draft at all.
  Solution: Either release the wool in the back hand, let it unwind and start again, or break off the over-twisted portion and start again. You will be surprised how strong the yarn is! Another solution is to treadle slower.
- The yarn is rapidly pulled out of your hands.
  Solution: Loosen the tension.
- The yarn kinks and curls and won't move onto the bobbin.
  Solution: Tighten the tension. Remember only a slight adjustment can make all the difference.
- The fibre will not draft smoothly.
  Solution: The preparation may not have been done correctly. Look at the fibre supply. Is it full of lumps and tangles?
- The yarn keeps breaking because it doesn't have enough twist or may be too thin.
  Solution: Slow your hands down to allow more twist to enter the yarn, or allow more fibre into the drafting zone to make the yarn thicker. You can also treadle faster.

SHORT BACKWARD DRAFT

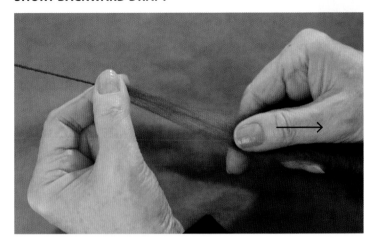

1.23 Follow the instructions in photos 1.18 and 1.19 (pages 24–25). As soon as the fibres have caught around the leader, draft back with the back hand while pinching with the front hand.

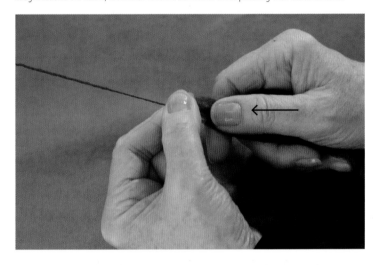

1.24 Bring your back hand towards the front hand while slightly releasing the pinch of the front forefinger and thumb to let the yarn move onto the bobbin. As the yarn runs onto the bobbin, it is smoothed by the gentle pressure of the front hand.

Don't be frustrated at your first efforts. It takes some coordination to have your feet treadling at the same speed as your drafting speed. In the beginning it is usual to find your hands are moving slower than your feet as you struggle to master the hand movements.

Usually the moment when you have got the speeds just right is quite sudden and you feel the harmony of your hands and feet moving together, not against each other. This moment is worth waiting for, as then you can understand why spinners talk about the meditative and soothing aspect of spinning.

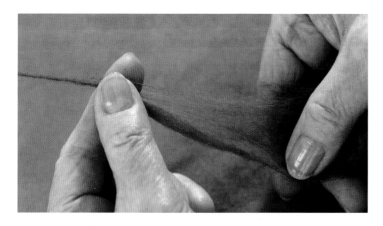

1.25 Hold the thinned-out, fluffy end of the fibre against the yarn. When it has caught onto the yarn, begin spinning as before.

1.26 Move the yarn along the flyer hooks frequently to prevent a build-up in one place. This also makes the yarn on the bobbin pack down more firmly; you can get more yarn on, and if you lose the end, it makes it easier to find. Remembering which hook the yarn disappeared from may also help you find this elusive end.

JOINING ON A NEW FIBRE SUPPLY

Some spinning wheels have a moveable hook, or you can have one fitted to your wheel. Again move this hook frequently. There is also a Woolee Winder, which has a gearing system added to the flyer which moves it automatically up and down the bobbin. It can be fitted to most makes of spinning wheels and makes for a very compact bobbin of spun yarn.

For your first attempt, do not try to completely fill the bobbin. Two half-filled bobbins will be enough.

PLYING

The wool on one bobbin is called a 'single'. This is an unbalanced yarn as it has been twisted all one way. There are uses for this type of yarn; in fact I wrote a book which concentrated on unbalanced yarn (*Collapse Weave: Creating Three-Dimensional Cloth*). If you knit with a

single yarn, the garment will have a slanted appearance. Singles can also be felted to give it stability, and washing will take out some of the twist as you can see in photo 1.27.

It is usual to ply two singles together. This makes the yarn stronger and more balanced. As you ply with the wheel turning anticlockwise, some of the twist is undone, then more is added in the opposite direction, and the plied yarn should have all the fibres running straight down the yarn length. It helps the singles to settle if you let them rest on the bobbin overnight before you begin plying. This will take out some of the kinks and curls.

1.27 Skeins of singles yarn, unwashed (left) and washed (right).

1.28 Put the two bobbins onto the lazy kate, facing the same way.

1.29 Place the lazy kate to one side and slightly behind you.

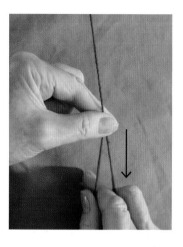

1.30 Take the ends from each of the bobbins and hold them against the leader with the forefinger and thumb of your front hand, allowing about a 10cm (4in) overlap. Your back hand rests on your hip, separating the two singles.

1.31 Begin treadling anticlockwise, pinching the two ends together with the leader until they have joined, then move the two singles towards the orifice.

1.32 Release the pinch slightly, enough to run your front hand down the two singles, following the twist down until your hands nearly meet.

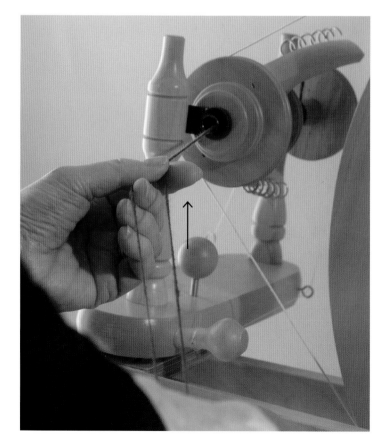

1.33 Tighten the pinch again and move the plied yarn towards the orifice. Repeat these last two movements. Because the plied yarn is thicker than the two singles, you may need to tighten the brake band to pull the yarn on at a steady rate.

1.34 Three different plied yarns. Test for the correct amount of twist by pulling some of the plied yarn off the bobbin. It should be evenly twisted and rounded in appearance (A). If there isn't enough twist the yarn looks flat and stringy (B). If it is over-plied, the yarn kinks and curls (C).

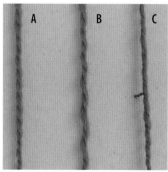

■ SKEINING

Using a niddy noddy is the easiest way to take the yarn off the bobbin ready for washing. If you run a strand of wool around your niddy noddy, you can measure how much will be on each turn, and then you will know how many metres or yards you have spun.

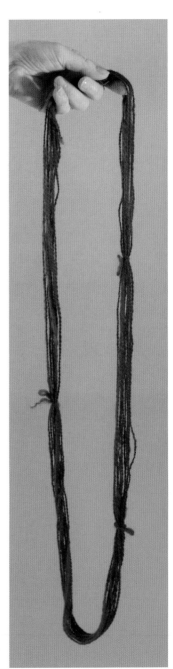

1.35 Loosen the brake band slightly, so the bobbin runs freely, stand over your wheel and take the end of the plied yarn and hold it against the niddy noddy upright with one hand.

1.36 With the other hand, wind the yarn around the niddy noddy, following the arrows. You can now see why it is called a niddy noddy.

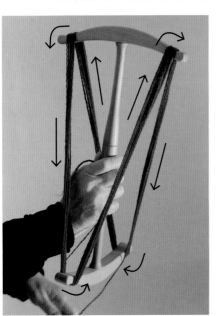

1.37 Tie the yarn in about four places, using the two ends, and then two other small pieces of yarn for the other two ties and remove it from the niddy noddy. When you hold it up, it should hang straight, although this may be too much to expect if this is your first skein.

Fig. 1 Z and S twist.

1.38 Z (left) and S (right) skeins.

1.39 Drying yarn.

BALANCED YARN

We spin the singles with the wheel turning clockwise, which gives the yarn a Z twist. We ply with the wheel turning anticlockwise to give the yarn an S twist. I used to get muddled about which was S and which was Z until a spinner told me that if you turn the wheel clockwise, your hand is moving in the same direction as the top stroke of the letter Z and if you turn the wheel anticlockwise, the wheel is turning in the same direction as the top stroke of the letter S.

If you have the twist count balanced between the spinning and the plying, the skein will hang straight, as in photo 1.37. The plied yarn should be spun with two-thirds of the twist of the singles. If the skein twists in an S direction (look at the direction of the diagonal), the yarn has too much twist in the singles compared to the plying and the skein is under-plied. If the skein twists in a Z direction, there is too much twist in the plying compared to the singles and the skein is over-plied.

A little bit of twisting in the skein when you take it off the niddy noddy is not important as the twist will disappear with washing. It is only if the skein twists several times that you need to think about how to remedy this next time. One very over-plied skein, I wound into a ball and ran back through with the spinning wheel turning clockwise to take out the extra twist.

■ WASHING

To set the twist and to let the yarn expand, it must be washed. Even wool that has been washed before spinning will need a second wash. The amount it will change with washing depends mainly on the fleece type. The yarn spun from some breeds of sheep, e.g., merino, will shrink in length and fluff up much more than coarser breeds like English Leicester. It also depends on how you have spun the yarn. Very tightly spun and plied yarn won't change as much as more loosely spun yarn.

31

Improving your first efforts

One word says it all: PRACTICE. Do lots of little skeins, wash and dry them and then have a good look to see what can be done better. Don't expect great yarn from the beginning, but learning to analyse your finished yarn will show you what needs to be done next time.

For this, your first spinning efforts, you have probably spun with clean carded wool. All you need to do is to soak your yarn in soapy water that is hot enough to get your hand into. Soak the skein for a few minutes, dunking it up and down a few times, but don't rub it. If you agitate it too much, it may felt. Then rinse it in warm water, wring it (you can roll it in a towel before wringing it) to get rid of excess water and hang the skein outside to dry. Don't use the spin cycle of a washing machine, unless you put the skein in a bag first, or dry in a tumble dryer.

If you have spun with greasy fleece, this will probably have more dust and dirt in it than the already prepared wool. In this case, soak it in warm water for an hour or two. If the wool is very dirty, you may need to change the water several times. Then wash it in the warm, soapy water as before. If you want to retain the grease, for a more waterproof yarn, wash in cold water.

■ CALCULATING THE AMOUNT OF YARN NEEDED FOR EACH PROJECT

If you have wound a length of yarn around your niddy noddy and then taken it off and measured it, as I suggested earlier, you can calculate how many metres/yards in each skein. For example, my niddy noddy measures 152cm (5ft) for one complete turn. If I have 50 turns, the skein will measure 76m (83yds). Remember that your yarn will shrink when it is washed, so make allowances for this.

I also note the weight of my skeins. All the projects in this book will give you the weight of the finished article.

Problem solving

- Your yarn is lumpy and bumpy, with some thin parts.
  Solution: Don't worry too much at this stage. The yarn will be more consistent with practice.
- Your yarn kinks and curls and is over-twisted in either the spinning or the plying.
  Solution: Tighten the tension on the brake band or treadle slower.
- The yarn is too thin and breaks.
  Solution: Add more wool into the drafting zone to make the yarn thicker.
- The spinning wheel moves away from you as you treadle.
  Solution: It may be that the drive band is too tight. Loosen it slightly. It can also be caused by your treadling feet/foot pushing away rather than down. Move your feet/foot further up the treadle. This happens more on a slippery floor, so a rubber mat under your wheel may help.
- The bobbin and/or flyer do not revolve easily.
  Solution: Check the maiden uprights. If they not parallel and are angled towards the bobbin, they cause drag.
- The flyer (on a flyer-led wheel) or the bobbin (on a bobbin-led wheel) does not turn when you treadle.
  Solution: Tighten the drive band.
- The yarn doesn't pull onto the wheel.
  Solution: Check that the yarn is not snagged around the hooks or caught around the spindle shaft.

■ PROJECTS

Knitted scarf

Once you have become an experienced spinner, you will find it difficult to spin the same type of yarn you have just finished — your first few skeins. They have a texture you may never achieve again. And the more you spin, the finer your yarn becomes. So make the most of this beginner yarn in the following projects.

The yarn I used in this knitted scarf is some of my daughter's first attempts. She kept producing skeins which I dismissed as they weren't bad enough! This was the worst she could manage. There is no need to make fancy stitches; the yarn adds all the interest needed.

Needle size: 12mm (US 17, UK 000), very large.

Stitch: Garter stitch

Cast on 30 sts. Knit in garter stitch for the required scarf length, then cast off.

Woven runner
by Anne Field

After nearly 50 years of trying to improve my spinning, I found it very difficult to spin this 'textured' yarn. However, I concentrated very hard and this is the result.

I use this surface weave structure frequently as the fancy yarns sit on the cloth surface, with the background yarn providing the necessary stability. The unevenness of the yarn doesn't matter, in fact it adds to the surface interest. The back of the cloth is neater but is also interesting. The size of the runner is based on a system which gives a length proportional to the width. The width is two-thirds of the length and always looks in proportion.

A surface weave structure has a textured weft yarn which lies on the surface of the fabric, while a second, thinner, weft yarn weaves a plain background underneath. This project could also be woven on a rigid heddle loom, using pick-up sticks for the surface weave areas.

Structure: Surface weave

Equipment: 4 shaft loom, 40cm (16in) wide, two shuttles. 8 dent reed

Warp yarn: Linen, 2 threads wound as one. Wraps per 2.5cm (1in): 32 of the doubled yarn. A cotton or cotton/linen mix yarn would also be suitable. See page 41 for a description of wraps per 2.5cm (1in).

Warp length: 1 runner 53cm (21in) long, plus 10cm (4in) fringe each end

Loom waste: 60cm (24in)

Total length of warp: 133cm (53in). 224 ends

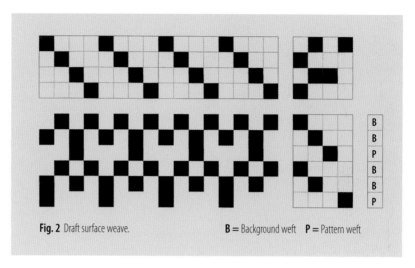

Fig. 2 Draft surface weave.   B = Background weft   P = Pattern weft

Weft yarn

Background: same as warp

Pattern yarn: Textured handspun 50m (54yds)

Width in reed: 36cm (14in)

Sett: 16 ends per 2.5cm (1in). 2 per dent in 8 dent reed

Picks per 2.5cm (1in): 16

Weight of finished runner: 90gm (3¼oz)

Weaving

Weave plain weave for 2.5cm (1in), using only the background yarn, hemstitch the end, then follow the draft. I didn't take the pattern yarn right to the selvedges but stopped 2.5cm (1in) each side as this makes a border. When the runner measures 53cm (21in), weave with plain weave and the background yarn only for 2.5cm (1in). Hemstitch.

I always weave slightly longer than I want the finished length to be as the weaving will contract when it comes off the loom. Linen does not shrink so I allowed for that in the woven length.

Twist the fringes. Wash the runner in warm soapy water, rinse, and dry lying flat. Press on the wrong side as this won't flatten the texture on the right side.

SOURCES

Woolee Winder: www.thewooleewinder.com

Ashford equipment: www.ashford.co.nz

Wheels & how they work

2.1 Traditional wheel, with overlay of flyer whorl (A) and drive wheel (B).

IN CHAPTER 1 we learnt enough about wheels to get you spinning! This chapter will go into more detail. As your spinning improves, you will want to spin different types of yarn, and this means controlling your wheel so it does what you want. In the beginning you probably feel as if the wheel has a mind of its own and you are just along for the ride.

When I first started spinning, I spun one yarn, a medium weight, two-ply yarn. This was all my first wheel, made out of a Singer sewing-machine wheel, could spin. Because the drive wheel was quite small, one turn of the drive wheel put four twists into the fibre I was drafting onto the bobbin, although I did not know any of this at the time. There were no books to explain how a spinning wheel worked. A year or so later I bought my first 'proper' wheel. This had a much larger drive wheel, and unknown to me, one turn of the drive wheel put 11 twists into the drafted wool. It took me months to work out that I had to spin thinner yarn for the greater amount of twist.

DETERMINING THE DRIVE RATIO OF YOUR WHEEL

Even if you were given this information when you bought your wheel, it helps to understand the principle of drive ratio by doing the following exercise. If you have a second-hand spinning wheel, you will need to do this exercise to find out the different drive ratios of your wheel.

■ DRIVE RATIO

Thinner yarn needs more twist than thicker yarn, otherwise it will break. It seems so obvious now but at the time this factor caused me great frustration. The amount of twist that goes into your yarn is governed by the drive ratio of your wheel. This ratio is the difference between the circumference of the drive wheel and the circumference of the flyer or bobbin whorl. Anything that sounds even vaguely mathematical is often daunting to new spinners, but there are practical ways to find the drive ratio of your wheel without any maths.

On flyer-led wheels, the drive wheel is connected to the flyer by the drive band (see photo 1.7, page 17). Each complete turn of the larger drive wheel causes the flyer whorl to revolve a greater number of times. This is because the flyer whorl is smaller in circumference.

On bobbin-led wheels, the drive wheel is connected via the drive band to the bobbin (see photo 1.16, page 23), which has a smaller whorl.

The bigger the difference between the drive wheel and the whorl, the quicker the flyer or bobbin turns and the more twist goes into the yarn. Each time the flyer or bobbin makes a complete circle, one twist is put into the yarn feeding onto the bobbin. This is why my small Singer sewing-machine wheel could only put in four twists while my second wheel, with a larger drive wheel, could put in 11, even although the flyer whorls were probably the same size.

2.2 Detail of double-drive bobbin and flyer whorls.

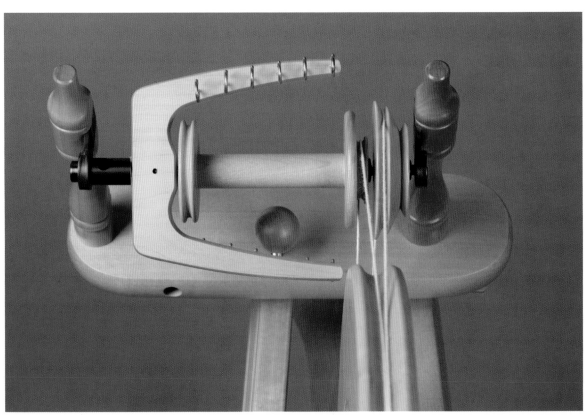

2.3 Footman and flyer lined up.

The first spinning wheels made when spinning became popular in the 1970s had only one flyer or bobbin whorl size. Now most wheels have several interchangeable whorls. If you have a new wheel, the information that came with your wheel will tell you the various drive ratios. They are written as 6.1, or 10.1, meaning one turn of the drive wheel will give you 6 or 10 revolutions of the flyer or bobbin and put 6 or 10 twists into the amount of yarn fed on.

Double-drive wheels (see photo 1.17, page 23) have a doubled drive band, with one half of the band going around the bobbin whorl and the other half going around the flyer whorl. The bobbin whorl is smaller than the flyer whorl so the bobbin goes faster than the flyer. The two whorls have a different shaped groove: the bobbin whorl groove is U-shaped and the flyer whorl is V-shaped. This allows for some slippage on the bobbin so you can hold the yarn back while spinning to allow the twist to build up.

On the bobbin and flyer-led wheels, this slippage occurs because the brake and drive bands, being separate, are made of different types of thread. The brake band is usually a slippery material like nylon while the drive band is string or something similar which has some grip. If the bobbin and flyer revolve at the same speed, the yarn will not pull onto the bobbin.

Flyer-led and double-drive wheels
Tie a short piece of yarn to one arm of the flyer and line up this arm with the footman, the connection between the treadle and the drive wheel, so the footman is at the top of its crank.

Turn the wheel slowly by hand, counting the number of times the flyer revolves, until the footman returns to its original position. Round it up or down; do not worry about half or quarter revolutions. If the flyer turns 6 times, this is your drive ratio.

2.4 Flyer with three whorls.

Bobbin-led wheel

Mark your bobbin with a small piece of sticky tape and then count the number of times the bobbin goes around to one turn of the drive wheel. This is your drive ratio.

Do this exercise with all the different whorls. On the flyer-led wheels, the flyer may have two or more whorls as part of the flyer; on double drive-wheels, the whorls are attached to the spindle that holds the flyer. On bobbin-led wheels, the bobbin itself will have different sized whorls.

REGULATING THE TWIST

Now we know the drive ratios of your wheel, we can regulate the amount of twist you can put into your yarn, by feeding in a pre-determined length of yarn in each draft. This takes some practice. If my drive ratio is 9, and I feed 2.5cm (1in) of yarn onto the bobbin for one treadle push, I will be putting 9 twists into that 2.5cm (1in). This is very jerky, and it is easier to feed in 5cm (2in) to two treadle pushes. Remember one treadle push equals one turn of the drive wheel and 9 turns of the flyer/bobbin.

It is easier to spin with the twist count and drive ratio as close as possible. If you want to spin a yarn with 9 twists to 2.5cm (1in), choose a drive ratio of as near 9 as possible. Otherwise you are making hard work of spinning. For example, if I want to spin a yarn with 9 twists and my drive ratio is 5, I will have to feed in nearly 2.5cm (1in) of yarn to two pushes of the treadle. This is hard work. This means my feet are working twice as quickly as my hands.

If I want to spin with 5 twists to 2.5cm (1in), and my drive ratio is 9, I will have to draft twice as quickly as my feet are treadling.

IN CHAPTER 1, I told you about the difference in twists per 2.5cm (1in) between single and plied yarn. Plied yarn is spun with two-thirds less twist than the singles. Therefore, sometimes it helps to change the whorls when plying.

All spinners will tell you the reason they love to spin is because it is so relaxing, a meditative process that soothes the mind and body. If your hands and feet are not working in unison, you lose this state of mind, and spinning can become tiring and lose its charm. I find I can spin with one or two more or less twists to the centimetre (or inch) than my drive ratio by adjusting the length of the draft slightly. If the difference becomes any bigger, I change whorls.

The rhythm of my hands and feet are a very important part of my spinning. I have even been known to fall asleep spinning. In the early days, when most wheels only had one whorl, some of us used that as an excuse to buy other wheels with different drive ratios to suit different-sized yarns. Not that we need much excuse. I once stayed with a spinner who had 30 wheels in her house. She even had one in her bathroom.

The appearance of our wheels is also important. We like them to be a thing of beauty, as this also helps put us in the right mood for spinning. A wheel that clanks or squeaks can also ruin this mood.

Try to buy a wheel that has at least two different drive ratios as these different whorl sizes make it easy to spin a variety of yarn sizes.

▍ MEASURING YARN SIZE

Because the size of the yarn and the twist count are important, we do need a way of measuring the size of various yarns. We do this by wrapping the yarn around a ruler for 2.5cm (1in) and counting the number of wraps. Don't stretch the yarn, as this thins it out, and make sure the yarns touch each other. This will be the way the yarns are sized for the projects in this book. This method can be used for singles, and two- or three-ply yarn. When yarn is plied, it doesn't double in size but increases by about 50%.

For projects, particularly if you need to spin a lot of yarn, it is helpful to take a length of the spun singles off the bobbin when you think you have the correct size for your project, let it double back on itself, and attach this yarn to your spinning wheel. Next time you begin spinning you can measure this sample against your latest spinning to see if they match. If not, adjust your spinning accordingly.

It is best to spin all the yarn for one project before you begin the knitting or weaving because the size can change with different

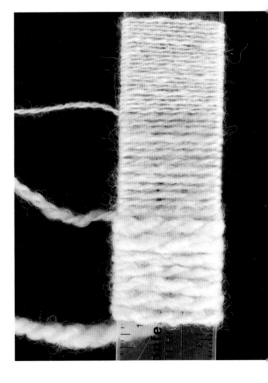

2.5 Wraps.

41

2.6 From left: fine (alpaca) spun by Bev Tilson; medium (wool); thick (wool) spun by Margaret Stewart.

spinning sessions, even if you are using the same fibre. One impatient spinner I taught began knitting a jersey with her first skein. By the time she had reached the shoulder of the jersey, her spinning was half the size of the original and much improved. So the ribbing at the lower end of that garment was thick and lumpy while the shoulder yarn was much improved. So choose small projects with your first yarns.

I have divided yarn into three sizes:
- Fine: 20+ wraps per 2.5cm (1in)
- Medium: 8–19 wraps
- Thick (sometimes called bulky): less than 8 wraps

For a well-rounded yarn, the wraps are usually twice the twists, e.g., a yarn with 8 wraps to 2.5cm (1in) should have 4 twists per 2.5cm (1in). Weavers often put more twist into their yarn as they want a strong, abrasion-resistant yarn, especially for warps. Knitters may want a softer yarn with less twists as the knitting process adds slightly more twist.

SPINNING FINE YARN

For fine yarn, use the smallest whorl as this will give you more twists. For example, if you want to spin a yarn with 15 twists to 2.5cm (1in), then choose a drive ratio as close to this as possible. Then your hands and feet are moving in harmony. When changing to a smaller whorl from a larger whorl, the drive band will become looser unless it is one of the stretchy polyurethane drive bands. With a string drive band, there is an adjustment knob which moves the mother-of-all further away from the

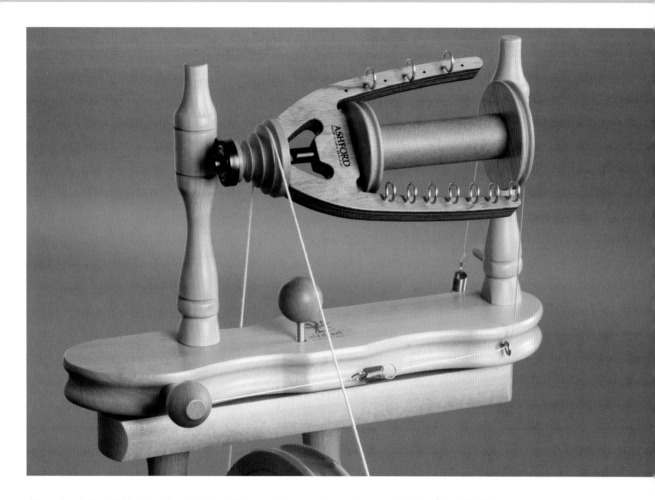

2.7 Lace flyer and bobbin.

drive wheel, thus tightening the drive band. Some spinners, when using a string cord drive band, have two drive bands, one shorter than the other, and the spare band is tied around the wheel upright when not in use. The shorter band is used with the smaller whorls for finer spinning. This does save tedious retying of drive bands when you change whorls and the drive-band adjustment doesn't have enough leeway.

If you are spinning fine wool yarn, it is also best to choose a sheep breed that produces fine wool (see photos 4.4 and 4.5, pages 89 and 90). If you are spinning with other fibres, such as alpaca or mohair, again choose the finer fibres.

Draft less fibre to make the yarn finer and have a light tension on your brake band. If you have a double-drive wheel, the drive band shouldn't be too tight. For very fine yarn, a lace flyer will help. This has small whorls and holds a bobbin with a thicker centre core than the usual bobbins.

Remember that you will ply with less twists than you put into the single yarn. For example, if you spin with 15 twists to 2.5cm (1in), then you should ply with 10 twists.

This fine yarn would be suitable for scarves, shawls and baby wear.

SPINNING MEDIUM YARN

A drive ratio of about 6–8 is suitable for medium yarn, which I would use for jerseys and sweaters, hats, mittens and gloves. I would choose a wool from the breeds such as in photos 4.6 and 4.7 (pages 91 and 92). When spinning with fibres other than wool, choose slightly thicker fibres.

This is probably the most common type of yarn spun, as it has many practical uses, therefore most wheels have at least one drive ratio in this range. Allow more fibre into the drafting zone as you spin.

SPINNING THICK YARN

A drive ratio of between 3–6 is suitable for thicker yarn as the strong fibres have enough strength and don't need a lot of twist. Indeed, if you put a lot of twist into thick wool, the yarn will be very heavy and inflexible. If spinning with wool, suitable breeds are those in photo 4.8 (page 93).

Bobbin-led wheels are often preferred for this type of spinning, as the bobbin fills quickly and the drive wheel, turning the bobbin instead of the flyer, can manage the heavier workload. They often have larger bobbins, too, which can hold more yarn. A large orifice helps, as do larger hooks to prevent this thicker wool catching. Some spinners use a thicker drive band as this gives more traction.

A jumbo flyer, with a large orifice and hooks, also makes spinning thicker yarn easier. They come with larger bobbins and have a drive ratio of 4.5–9.

2.8 Jumbo flyer.

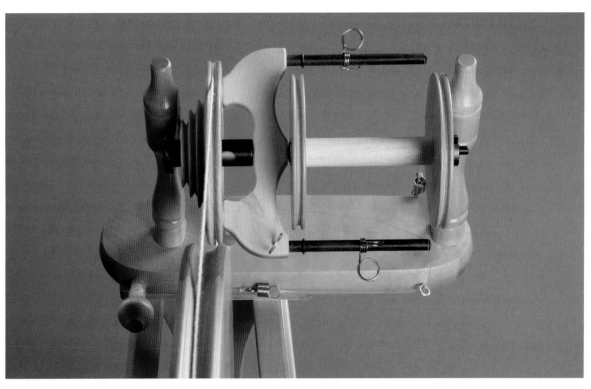

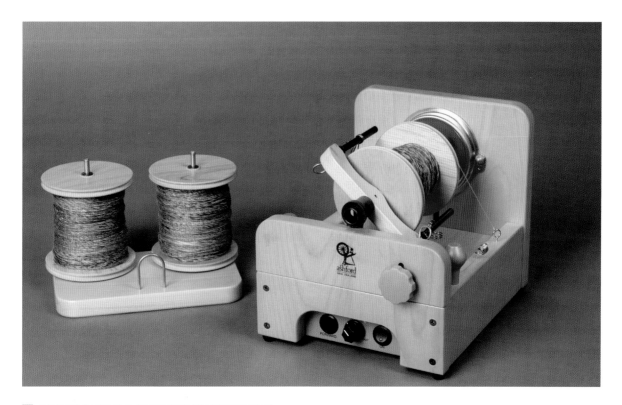

ELECTRONIC SPINNING WHEELS

An electronic spinning wheel has a variable range, not a fixed drive ratio, so can be used for a wide variety of yarns. These wheels usually have larger bobbins, which makes them suitable for thicker wool, but fine wool can also be spun on them.

If you have trouble treadling, these wheels are for you as the motor does all the work. They are also very portable. Early electronic and electric spinning wheels used to be very noisy and I can remember teaching years ago and finding these wheels irritating. I can also remember the time spent trying to find the nearest power point. However, the newer wheels are very quiet.

WHEEL MAINTENANCE

It is important to look after your wheel. The moving parts should be oiled frequently and a good wax polish will protect the wood. Wheels are so lovely to look at that some people have them just as a piece of furniture, but spinners want to do more than admire them and a smoothly running wheel will add to your enjoyment.

My second wheel, which I spun on for about 35 years, needed a new flyer after about 20 years as I actually wore a groove right through the flyer. So check your wheel regularly for wear and tear.

Many of the older wheels had nylon bearings, which needed oiling frequently. Newer wheels have ball bearings, which don't need to be oiled, so check to see what is on your wheel.

2.9 Electronic spinning wheel.

2.10 Elizabeth wheel with oil points:
A) bobbin bearings; B) flyer bearings; C) wheel bearings; D) conrod bearings; E) treadle pins.

2.11 (opposite page) Upright Ashford Traveller wheel.

▓ WHICH WHEEL IS BEST FOR YOU

If possible, try out various wheels before you purchase your own. This will give you some idea of which wheels you are more comfortable with. Try both double- and single-treadle wheels. A double-treadle wheel spreads the workload between both feet and may be better for you.

Upright wheels usually have smaller drive wheels, as the orifice has to be at hand height. They are easy to carry but you will need to treadle faster than on a Saxony-type wheel, where the wheel is to the side of the flyer and can be larger.

2.12 Tension knob on double-drive wheel.

SCOTCH-TENSION WHEELS (See photo 1.15, page 22)

These are the most common single-drive wheels and you can adjust the brake band easily. The brake band and the drive band are separate, and this allows you to adjust them one at a time. Generally, this helps beginners, whose lumpier yarn needs more tension to be pulled onto the bobbin. However, if you choose a wheel that has both double-drive and Scotch-tension options, you have the best of both wheels. Many beginners prefer the double-drive option when their spinning improves.

IRISH-TENSION WHEELS (See photo 1.16, page 23)

Because these wheels have the drive band around the bobbin, they are well suited for spinning thick yarn, as the bobbins, which are usually large, hold a lot of yarn and become heavy when full. As the drive band, which has good traction because it has contact with the large surface area of the drive wheel, drives the bobbin, not the flyer, there is plenty of pull even with a full bobbin.

DOUBLE-DRIVE WHEELS (See photo 2.10, page 46)

As the drive and brake bands are a single, doubled band, there is less adjustment possible. A very small tightening or loosening of the band will make a difference to both the brake and drive-band tension. Once the tension has been set, it won't move and I find the tension on these wheels is more consistent. Sometimes the vibration can loosen the brake-band knob on a Scotch-tension wheel and the tension changes as you spin. This is particularly so with older wheels where the brake knob may be worn.

With this double-drive system, all the action is positive; that is, all the parts — flyer, bobbin and drive wheel — are moving. With the Scotch and Irish tension, the flyer and bobbin are slowed down by the brake band.

SOURCE

Ashford equipment: www.ashford.co.nz

Problem solving

- The knob that controls the brake band can become loose with wear. This is frustrating as the brake band gradually unwinds and the yarn won't run onto the bobbin.
  Solution: Replace with a new brake knob
- If the drive band keeps coming off the flyer or bobbin whorl, or comes off the drive wheel itself, check that the band runs in a straight line from the drive wheel to the whorl.
  Solution: Adjust the mother-of-all so the whorl and the groove on the drive wheel are lined up. This involves moving the mother-of-all to the correct position.
- Hooks. These can become worn with time and will roughen and snag the yarn.
  Solution: Replace the hooks.
- The orifice can become clogged with grease and dirt.
  Solution: Clean with a cotton bud soaked in methylated spirits.
- Sometimes we acquire bobbins that are older and do not revolve easily around the shaft.
  Solution: Try applying oil to the shaft. If this isn't enough, the centre of the bobbin may be reamed out with a round file or some sandpaper wrapped around a pencil if the bobbins are the older type without the plastic inserts at each end.
- Drive band. Any band will stretch with time and wear, causing slippage.
  Solution: If the band is cotton, bring the mother-of-all to its closest position to the drive wheel. Tie on a new cord using a reef knot, or splice the ends together. Do not leave long ends dangling or make a big, lumpy knot. If the band is one of the stretchy polyurethane ones, replace with a new stretchy band.
- Squeaky wheels are very irritating. In one class I sat on the floor beside a squeaky wheel to locate the source.
  Solution: Oil is the first thing to try. If this does not work, try to find the offending joint and check it is not rubbing against something. If it is, you may need to loosen the joint so there is a gap.
- The spring at the end of the brake band can lose its stretch after a time.
  Solution: Replace with a new spring or a rubber band.

Other ways to spin

FOR 30 YEARS I spun one type of yarn. I became very good at it but it had a limited use. It was medium-weight yarn, spun worsted (although I didn't know this term at the time). This yarn was suited to the long-wool breed of sheep which New Zealand had in abundance, my wheel spun it easily and it was the right weight for the garments I was making at the time. These were mainly outdoor jerseys for the family or blankets and throws. Most spinners have one type of yarn they do best and I could almost spin this yarn in my sleep.

When I first began to spin, I had one wheel and no carders or combs to prepare the only source of fibre, wool, which I bought as fleeces straight from the farm or from wool stores. I sold most of my spun yarn and this medium-weight wool was practical and sold easily. Handspun wool was seen as a hard-wearing, almost waterproof yarn, so it was purchased for knitting into outdoor jerseys. The only dyes available were plant dyes. I began to spin in the 1960s and in the late '60s and '70s the world was into all things natural — a return to the simple things of life. Everyone was into crafts like macramé, cane work, weaving and spinning.

Eventually I wanted to make different garments. I acquired more spinning wheels with different drive ratios and started travelling overseas to teach, where I saw a much wider range of sheep breeds and other fibres. But it was difficult to break the habits of all those years. This chapter will teach you other methods of preparation and spinning. Thus the range of yarn you can produce is endless and suited to almost anything you would want to make.

Another change over the years is that I now buy much of my fibre already prepared for me by commercial mills. With this fibre there is no waste so, although the initial cost is usually higher than buying raw fleeces, in the long run the cost is about the same. I can also save time as the preparation has been done for me. Throughout this book I will discuss both raw fibre and the commercial preparations, and how to use each. But there is nothing to beat the satisfaction of seeing the animals and then the resulting fleeces. When our guild visits farms, we always come home with bags of fibre that we want but don't really need!

You can see from photo 3.1 the difference in worsted and woollen yarn, and there are many intermediary types of yarn that have some of the qualities of one or the other. Also each spinner brings their own skills and dexterity to their yarn, so no two spinners will ever produce exactly the same yarn. I can teach a class of 20 spinners to spin worsted, and each one will produce a different yarn although they are using the same fibre and tools.

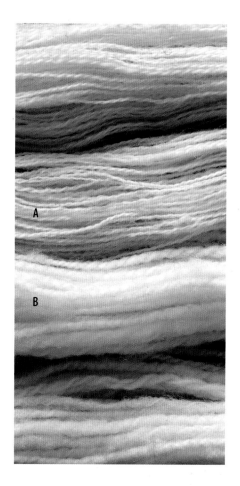

3.1 Worsted (A) and woollen (B) yarn.

Because I spun worsted yarns for so long, I will always be a better worsted spinner. Most experienced spinners have a favourite type of yarn they spin best, but as a beginner spinner, try other ways of spinning once you have mastered the basics. You will also learn more about the capabilities of your spinning wheel and what you enjoy spinning the most.

This chapter is about the preparation and spinning of wool; other fibres will be covered in later chapters. Washing and drying of these yarns is covered on pages 31–32.

■ WORSTED SPINNING

Choose your fibre wisely. Worsted yarn is spun from animals that have a long staple length of at least 10cm (4in). This includes the long-wool sheep, such as Romney, English Leicester, Lincoln, and Coopworth; also mohair and alpaca if the staple is long enough, and silk and flax.

PREPARATION

A worsted yarn has parallel fibres. Therefore, before you can start spinning, the fibres need to be prepared so they lie parallel. Sheep, alpacas and goats grow their fibres neatly in such a parallel formation for us. If we spin directly from the raw fibre, straight from the animal's back, the fibres are already correctly lined up, and we need to do

3.2 Tops and roving.

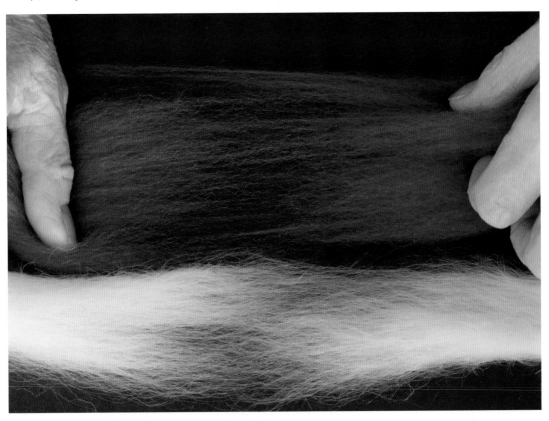

3.3 Long-stapled Romney fleece wool.

nothing more to straighten them out. But animals live outside in most weathers and their coats can become matted or contaminated with dirt, dust, vegetable matter and other nasties. The amount of preparation depends on the state of the raw material. Newly shorn, well-managed and clean animals have fibre that is a joy to spin, but we are not often lucky enough to be able to spin straight after shearing. I once stored a fleece for so long there was a bee's nest in it when I opened it out!

Some method of preparation is usual with most fibres. There is much debate about the merits of spinning with washed or unwashed fibre. Forty-five years ago I had many excellent sheep fleeces to choose from as New Zealand had about 60 million sheep, so I only chose clean fleeces I could spin in the grease (without washing first). For spinning worsted wool yarn, I still prefer to spin in the grease as this seems to make a smoother, more even yarn. Other fibres, such as alpaca and angora, contain no grease but the fibres may be contaminated with dirt and vegetable matter.

COMMERCIALLY PREPARED FIBRE

If you are buying the fibre already prepared, choose tops or combed roving as these have been carded, then combed to remove any short fibres and to make the fibres parallel. Tops are a preparation of commercial fibres which have been carded, then combed and have no twist. Rovings can be combed or carded and have a slight twist.

CHARACTERISTICS OF WORSTED SPINNING

- Hard-wearing.
- Solid, with little loft or springiness.
- The fibres are parallel and even in length.
- Little air is trapped in the yarn.
- It will not pill (pilling is the formation of loose fibres that rise to the surface with wear, forming little balls).
- The twist is evident.
- Lustrous.
- Doesn't change much with washing.
- Long fibres.

You can check to see how the fibre has been prepared by holding the prepared fibres up to the light and gently pulling them apart. The fibres should all run lengthways and will be smooth and almost slippery when you run your hands down them. Break the tops or roving lengthwise into strips about 15–20cm (6–8in) long.

PREPARING THE FIBRE YOURSELF

Serious worsted spinners advocate using English wool combs for preparing the fibres. These combs consist of four to eight rows of long, sharp metal teeth (tines) set into a wooden backing. They have long handles and each comb can weigh about 1–2kg (2–4lb).

Mini-combs are a better for beginner spinners to start with as they produce a long, thin roving which has been elongated (pre-drafted). The heavier wool combs do produce the smoothest and most parallel fibres, but for a beginner the mini-combs, flick carder or a metal comb are a good start.

3.4 These mini-combs have one row of tines but there are combs with two, three or four rows. For fine fibre, the tines need to be close together.

Carding with mini-combs

3.5 Load the staples onto the tines of a mini comb one staple at a time, with the cut end attached as shown. Two layers are enough.

3.6 Take the loaded comb in one hand (my left hand in the photo) and hold the empty comb in the other hand. Begin by passing the empty comb on its side at right angles through the fibre. The first pass should just comb the tips, the next pass goes deeper, and so on until most of the fibre is transferred to the empty comb. The tines shouldn't touch. Reverse these directions if you are left-handed.

3.7 Remove any wastage left on the almost empty comb. Push the fibre on the other comb up off the tines slightly.

3.8 Change hands so the full comb is again in the left hand. Repeat the passes again. Two or three transfers are usually enough.

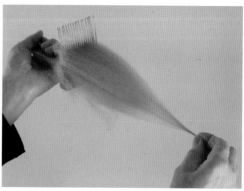

3.9 Pull and stroke the fibre tips together from the loaded comb and draw the fibre towards you as in pre-drafting. If you attach the comb to a fixed surface (my combs have a hook for this purpose), you can use both hands alternately.

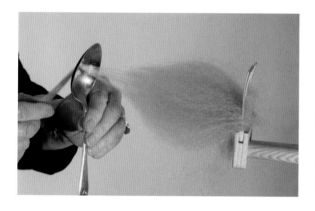

3.10 You can use a diz (a small curved shape with a hole in the middle) for this pre-drafting. This diz was made from a spoon.

3.11 Wind the pre-drafted fibre into a loose ball, giving it a slight twist as you do so. I have seen spinners simply attach the loaded comb to their belt and spin directly from that.

Problem solving

- The fibre does not move easily from the loaded comb to the empty comb.
  Solution: You are passing the empty comb too close to the tines. Remember to start by combing the tips first.
- The tines begin to bend.
  Solution: Again you may be passing the empty comb too deep into the fibres for the first few passes. You may also have too much fibre on the comb. If the tines are fine and close together, the fibre may be too coarse. Fine fibre needs fine and closely spaced tines. Coarse fibres need thicker, stronger tines.
- The fibres fold over on the moving comb.
  Solution: Give the comb a flick away from you to straighten out the fibres as you make the passes. Also make the passes larger, in a circular motion.

3. 12 Flick carder.

Carding with a flick carder

This is probably the most common tool, as it is inexpensive and easy to use. It is used for aligning fibres from sheep fleeces (washed or unwashed), alpaca and mohair. The fibres need to be 10cm (4in) or more in length. To flick card successfully, the fibres need to be parallel so if you are using washed fibre, try not to disturb the staple formation when washing. Don't take too much fibre at once. It is quicker to comb small amounts.

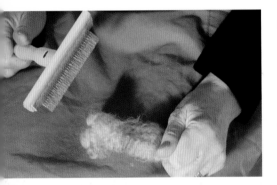

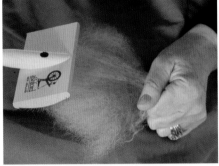

3.14 Hit down on the fibre with the flick carder, taking care to hit the fibre and not your other hand. Inexperienced spinners handling flick carders usually have pin pricks all over their hands. It is mainly the tips that need opening. As you continue tapping the fibres, they will fan out. Turn the fibre over and continue to open the other side.

3.13 Place a piece of cloth or leather on your lap. Hold the fibre tightly at the cut end in one hand on your lap and take the flick carder in the other hand.

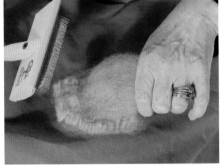

3.15 When the tip end is combed, reverse the fibre and, holding the fibre by the combed tip, open the cut end. Usually this doesn't need much work. There will be waste fibre left on the flick carder so remove this now and then with a comb.

Problem solving

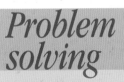

• The fibres end up tangled and pull out of your hand.
Solution: Hold the fibre tighter. You may also have tried to comb too much at once or you are dragging the metal teeth through the fibres, instead of tapping.

3. 16 Flick-carded fibre.

Carding with a metal comb

A metal comb can also be used in the same way as a flick carder. If the fibre is already open, a quick flick of the comb through the tip of the fibre may be all that is needed.

SPINNING METHOD

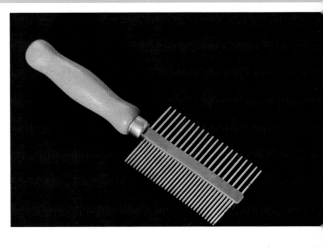

3.17 Metal comb.

For worsted spinning, we use the short forward or backward draft demonstrated in Chapter 1, photos 1.18 to 1.24 (pages 24–26). To keep the fibres parallel before drafting, hold them in their parallel formation in your back hand, letting the fibre flow out.

Don't open and close the back hand, or fiddle with the fibre. With this worsted method of spinning, the twist isn't allowed to pass into the drafting zone, and this reduces the amount of air trapped in the yarn. This is one of the features of correctly spun worsted yarn.

When plying, pinch and run the front hand down the yarn to keep the yarn lustrous and smooth.

USES
Knitting

As worsted yarn is hard-wearing, it is used mainly for outdoor jerseys and jackets, blankets, rugs and embroidery threads such as those used in cross-stitch. Lace patterns, Aran and Fair Isle show up well with this yarn.

Weaving

3.18 Hold the cut end of the fibre tightly in one hand on the lap protector, and, as with the flick carder, just tap the comb down onto the tip of the fibre until it has fanned out. Turn the staple over to do the other side. The cut ends may also need a cursory comb.

Worsted yarn is very useful for weaving because it is strong enough as a warp yarn to resist the abrasion of the heddles and reed. Also, as it is a smooth yarn, it doesn't catch in the heddles or reed.

3.19 Fleece and carded sliver.

CHARACTERISTICS OF SEMI-WORSTED SPINNING

- Softer than worsted yarn.
- Has fibres that are not parallel, but jumbled together.
- Some loft or springiness.
- It will pill, especially if the fibre is short, and has lots of noils (small pieces of fibre).
- Will change slightly with washing.
- Not as hard-wearing as worsted.

▉ SEMI-WORSTED SPINNING

The fibre used in semi-worsted spinning can be shorter in length than the fibres used for worsted spinning, so sheep breeds with a shorter staple, such as merino and Corriedale, and fibres such as angora (rabbit fur) and short-stapled mohair can be used.

This is probably the most common spinning method. More and more spinners are using commercially prepared fibre, which is usually carded and therefore not suitable for worsted spinning, which uses the combed tops or roving. With this yarn we change the preparation, not the spinning method.

COMMERCIALLY PREPARED FIBRE

Choose fibre that has been carded, not combed, such as carded sliver. If you hold these fibre arrangements up to the light and gently pull them apart, you will see that the fibres are randomly arranged and of different lengths, and there may be some noils. There will be no wastage.

This carded sliver is from a Romney/Polwarth cross sheep. I chose the fleece at my local wool carders as I loved the colour, then watched as it was carded for me. Sometimes the sliver is gilled (put through a machine once or twice to thin and straighten the fibres). However, for a true woollen preparation, the fibre is just carded.

If you want the resulting yarn to be softer and fluffier, break the sliver up across the width and roll it into a rolag before you start spinning.

If you want the yarn to be smoother and flatter, break up the sliver/batt lengthwise into about 15–20cm (6–8in) lengths ready to start spinning (see photo 3.26).

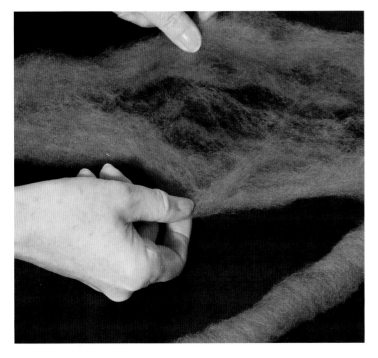

3.21 Place two smooth pieces of wood (plastic rulers are good for this) either side of the fibre.

3.20 Break up the sliver or batt.

3.22 Roll the fibre a couple of times around the rulers.

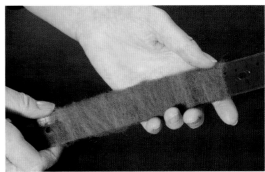

3.23 Break off the remaining fibre.

3.24 Smooth the fibres with your hand.

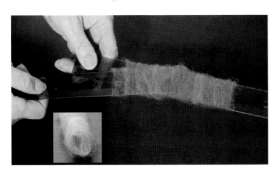

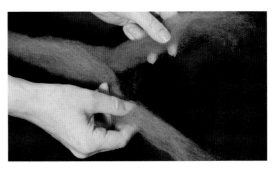

3.25 Remove the rulers one at a time.

3.26 Split the sliver/batt lengthwise.

3.27 Hand carders.

3.28 (right) Drum carder, doffer and brush.

PREPARING THE FIBRE YOURSELF

To make our own slivers or batts, use hand carders or drum carders. If you are doing small amounts at a time, hand carders will be suitable. However, if you have large amounts to prepare, a drum carder is very useful.

Both of these tools prepare the fibre so it is random and contains a lot of air. There is no wastage as all the fibres, short and long, are combined. Both hand and drum carders differ in the number of teeth set into the carding cloth. For fine fibres the carding cloth should have closer set and finer teeth; 108 points per square inch (ppsi). Hand carders are also available with 72 ppsi. The drum carder has 72 and 36 ppsi. For carding coarser fibres, 36 ppsi is enough.

Hand-carding

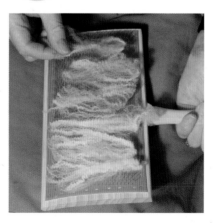

3.29 Place one of the carders on your lap, teeth upwards, and load on the fibres so they are parallel and just catching on the metal teeth. It may speed up the process if you tease apart any tips that are stuck together before you start. If the fibre is longer than the carder width, it is too long to be carded and may need to be cut in half. Don't overfill the carder as it is quicker to do lots of small amounts than to try to do large amounts.

Problem solving

Like most things your carding will get better and quicker with practice. If the fibre does not card properly here are some helpful hints.

• The fibre bends back over the carder.
Solution: Make sure the carders are further apart before you stroke one against the other. The fibre may also be too long. If it is longer than the width of the carder, cut it in half.

• The teeth grate against one another and it is hard work.
Solution: Separate the carders more when carding so the teeth are barely touching one another.

• Some of the fibre is still stuck together when you have finished.
Solution: You are trying to card too much fibre at once, or the fibres were too long.

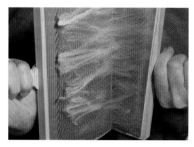

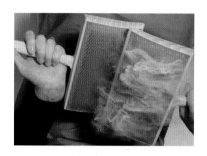

3.30 Hold the carders as shown with the filled carder in your left hand. This means you do not have to change your grip throughout the process. Brush the empty carder lightly across the filled carder. The first stroke should only brush the front one-third of each carder, the second two-thirds and the last stroke should cover the complete width. The teeth from each carder shouldn't catch on each other as you do this. About half the fibre should now be on the right carder.

3.31 The remaining uncarded fibre on the left carder is now stripped off onto the right carder. Turn the right carder over, teeth facing upwards, and place the toe (the end furthest away from the handle) of the left carder against the heel (the end nearest the handle) of the right carder. Bring the right carder swiftly up the left carder, lifting the fibre off the left carder onto the right.

3.32 This leaves all the fibre on the right carder.

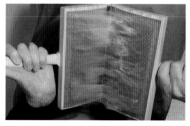

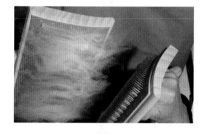

3.33 Hold the empty left carder face upwards, and stroke the right carder across it three times as before.

3.34 Now strip the right carder onto the left. Put the toe of the right carder against the heel of the left, the reverse of 3.31, and swiftly bring up the left carder so all the fibre is now on the left carder.

3.35 Hold the empty right carder face downwards and repeat the three strokes. Repeat the action in photo 3.31. Three exchanges are usually enough. All the fibre should now be on the right carder.

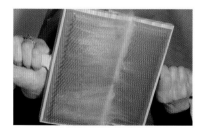

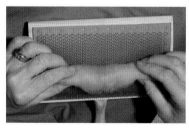

3.36 To remove all the fibre, place the toe of the empty left carder against the toe of the right carder and slightly under it and pull up the left carder to lift off the fibre. Then place the right carder under the left to lift the fibre off the left carder.

3.37 Roll the fibre up the teeth into a rolag ready for spinning.

3.38 There are many different ways of using hand carders, For example, if you want the fibre to be less random, roll the rolag down the length of the carders.

Drum-carding

For a soft, fluffier yarn, break the batt widthwise and make a rolag as described in photos 3.20–3.25 (page 59). You may need to halve the complete batt first as if there is too much fibre in each rolag, the fibre will not flow easily when you start spinning from it. For a slightly firmer yarn, strip the batt lengthwise as in photo 3.26 (page 59).

3.39 Tease the tips of the fibres apart and place them on the feed tray, just touching the small drum.

3.40 Turn the handle to draw the fibres in. Don't hold the fibres back on the feed tray as this will cause them to wrap around the small drum.

3.41 Continue feeding in fibre until the large drum is filled nearly to the top of the metal teeth.

3.42 To consolidate the batt, hold a long-haired brush (mine is a wallpaper brush) against the teeth of the large drum as you continue to turn the handle for a few turns. Some carders have a packer brush attached, which will do the same thing.

3.43 To remove the batt, turn the handle until the metal strip is at the top of the large drum. Place the doffer under the batt at this point and lift up the fibres in two or three stages to separate it. Do not cut the fibre off.

3.44 To remove the batt cleanly, place a cardboard tube with a strip of about three paper towels on it, under the separated fibres. Push the tube down onto the teeth and roll the batt off, with the drum turning in the opposite direction. This should leave no fibre remaining on the carder. Break the batt up into small portions and run them through the drum carder again. Two or three passes should be sufficient.

SPINNING METHOD

Again this is the short forward or backward draft as described in Chapter 1, photos 1.18–1.24 (pages 24–26). This yarn can be made softer or firmer depending on whether the batt is split widthwise (softer) or lengthwise (firmer) as described earlier in this chapter. Soft yarn will not be as hard-wearing as firmer yarn so think of your end use before you decide which method to use. You can smooth the yarn down when plying to make the yarn smoother and flatter, or lift your hand off the yarn for a fluffier surface.

USES
Knitting

Knit outdoor jerseys, hats, mittens and socks. Patterns won't show up as much as with worsted yarn.

Weaving

This yarn will make softer blankets and rugs than worsted yarn but is still suitable for a warp as well as a weft. It has more bulk and will be springier to handle than worsted yarn, but is not as hard-wearing. It is also useful for jacket and coat fabrics.

Problem solving

- The batt is not light and open, but portions are clumped together.
  Solution: The fibre was not opened sufficiently before it was placed on the feed tray.
- The fibres are catching on the small drum.
  Solution: You are holding them down on the feed tray or the large drum is too full.
- The fibres are catching around the axles, not the drum itself.
  Solution: You are feeding in the fibre too near the edges of the drum.
- The handle is very hard to turn.
  Solution: You are feeding in too much fibre at once, or the fibres aren't opened enough. The axles could also need oiling. The fibre could also be too long. If it is more than about 10cm (4in), cut it in half.
- The teeth on the two drums grate together as you turn the handle.
  Solution: The drums are too close together. Adjust them so they are slightly further apart. The distance between should be enough so a sheet of paper can be placed in-between.

CHARACTERISTICS OF WOOLLEN YARN

- It is soft and light.
- It is not hard-wearing and will matt and felt easily, although this does depend on the fibre used.
- The twist will not be very evident in the yarn.
- The yarn is rounded.
- There is a lot of air trapped in the yarn.
- It will pill.

■ WOOLLEN YARN

This is a soft, fluffy yarn spun from short, randomly arranged fibres. It is the only way I can spin short fibres such as cotton and the shorter down fleeces. This yarn has a marvellous loft as it contains so much air.

COMMERCIALLY PREPARED FIBRE

Choose carded sliver that has randomly arranged fibres, as in the sliver in photo 3.19 (page 58). For a lighter, softer yarn prepare the sliver as in photos 3.20–3.25 (page 59). A slightly firmer yarn is prepared as in photo 3.26 (page 59).

PREPARING THE FIBRE YOURSELF

This is done by hard-carding (see photos 3.29–3.38, pages 60–61) or by drum-carding (see photos 3.39–3.44, page 62). The shorter the fibres, the easier they are to randomly arrange, and the fluffier and softer your yarn.

SPINNING METHOD

For woollen spinning, we use the medium-draft or the long-draw method. Because the fibres need to draft easily, I recommend you use washed fibres, as greasy fibres may stick together while drafting.

Both these spinning methods produce woollen yarn but the long-draw method seems to make a lighter and airier yarn. When plying woollen-spun yarn, do not smooth the yarn down as this takes some of the air out.

Problem solving

- The yarn does not run onto the bobbin when you bring the yarn forward.

  Solution: Tighten the tension slightly. With this method of spinning, unlike worsted spinning, the tension is critical. You need enough tension to allow you to hold the yarn in place while drafting, but with enough pull so the yarn can feed onto the bobbin.

- The yarn breaks frequently.

  Solution: You are not allowing enough twist into the fibre as you draft.

- The fibres cannot draft.

  Solution: You are letting too much twist into the drafting areas and the fibres cannot move past each other.

- The yarn won't flow smoothly from the back hand.

  Solution: The fibre hasn't been prepared well enough. More carding may be needed.

Medium draft

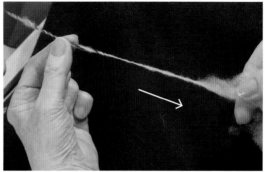

3.45 Hold the rolag in the back hand against the leader and pinch the leader and fibres together until they are joined.

3.46 Draft by pulling back with the back hand while keeping the front hand near the orifice, supporting the yarn, and ready to pinch if you feel you are losing control. It is crucial that you draft just as the fibres are beginning to twist.

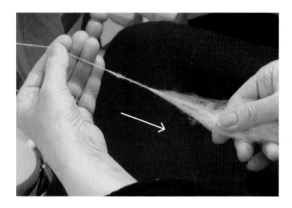

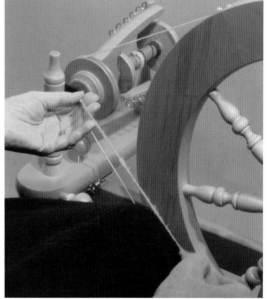

3.47 The back hand does all the work, drafting and opening and closing to let more fibre into the drafting zone.

3.48 You can draft back as far as it is comfortable for your arm to reach, or you can keep the drafting to a smaller area in front of your body.

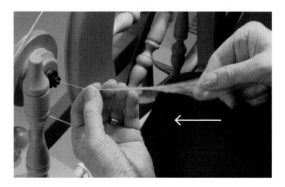

3.49 When the yarn is the correct size and twist, move the yarn onto the bobbin.

Long draw

3.50 Join the fibre onto the leader as normal, then draft back so there is a short length of spun fibre in front of your front hand. Now treadle three or four times, pinching the fibres where the twisted yarn meets the unspun fibre. This traps the twist, which gathers in front of the front hand.

3.51 The back hand holds the rolag, with a portion extending from that hand.

USES
Knitting

Woollen spun yarn is ideal for soft, light, airy garments, such as shawls and scarves, which won't be subjected to hard wear and lots of washing. It is also good for hats. Use larger needles than when knitting with worsted-type yarns as this encourages the light, fluffy appearance of the yarn. Patterns won't show up clearly.

Weaving

Again use for shawls and scarves but sett it further apart as otherwise the warp yarn will stick together and be difficult to separate. Complex patterns won't show up. This yarn will change, contract and fluff up more with washing.

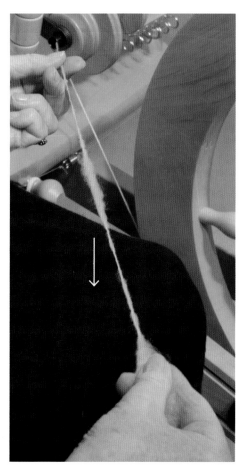

3.52 Ease the pinch of the front hand, at the same time drafting back with the back hand and letting the released twist run up until the extended portion of the fibre is loosely drafted. There should be just enough twist to hold this yarn together. Don't let any more fibre into the drafting zone.

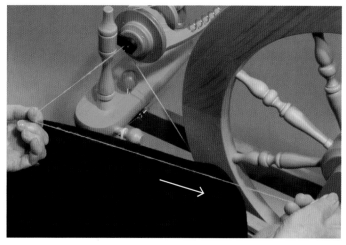

3.53 You should now have a loosely spun yarn, with some thinner, twisted areas and some thicker, less twisted areas. Control the amount of twist let into the yarn by opening and pinching with the front hand while elongating the length of yarn. The untwisted areas will slide past one another, making the yarn more even. The back hand pinches the yarn so no more fibre escapes. When the yarn is consistent, let the yarn length run onto the bobbin.

Problem solving

- The yarn breaks as you draft back with the back hand.
  Solution: You are moving the back hand back too fast and there isn't enough twist to hold it together.
- The fibre doesn't run smoothly from the rolag in the back hand.
  Solution: The fibre needs more preparation in the carding.
- The yarn doesn't run smoothly onto the bobbin.
  Solution: If the yarn is at too much of an angle as it enters the orifice, there is too much drag and friction. It is difficult to spin long draw on a wheel with a delta orifice, a V-shaped metal holder, as the yarn wobbles unless you are spinning with the yarn coming straight out from the V. Some wheels with a delta orifice can be angled so the yarn always spins from the tip. A 'pig tail' (a curly wire) orifice has the same effect.

CHARACTERISTICS OF
SEMI-WOOLLEN SPINNING

- The yarn won't pill, because all the short fibres and noils have been removed by combing.
- The fibres in the yarn will be parallel, again because of the combed preparation, and the yarn surface will be smooth.
- There will be some air in the yarn, and it will be springy and rounded with some bulk.
- It is more hard-wearing than woollen yarn, but not as hard-wearing as worsted or semi-worsted.
- It will full (mesh together when washed) reasonably well.
- The twist will not be clearly defined.

■ SEMI-WOOLLEN SPINNING

This yarn is not quite as soft and fluffy as woollen spun yarn and is more suited to long-staple fibres that are too long to hand- or drum-card. With these longer fibres, you can still spin a soft yarn.

COMMERCIALLY PREPARED FIBRE

This fibre should be in the form of tops or rovings, preparations that have been carded, then combed into a parallel formation with fibres of the same length. Break off no more than 15cm (6in) and split the fibre lengthwise so you are not holding too much in your hand.

PREPARING THE FIBRE YOURSELF

Use mini-combs (see photos 3.4–3.11, pages 54–55), flick carder or comb, as in photos 3.12–3.17 (pages 56–57).

SPINNING METHOD

Spin with the medium draft (see photos 3.45—3.49, page 65) or the long draw (see photos 3.50–3.53, pages 66–67).

USES
Knitting

Use this semi-woollen yarn for jerseys where you want a light, slightly fluffy yarn that will stand more wear and washing than woollen-spun garments.

Problem solving

- The fibres become tangled up and will not flow freely.
  Solution: Hold less fibre in the back hand, and hold it firmly enough so it flows freely and lets a controlled amount into the drafting zone. The fibres may also need more preparation. Keep the fibre parallel as you draft.
- The yarn breaks frequently as you let it pull onto the bobbin.
  Solution: Let more fibre into the drafting zone or allow more twist into the fibres as you draft.
- The yarn doesn't run onto the bobbin when you bring the yarn forward.
  Solution: Tighten the tension slightly. With this method of spinning, unlike worsted spinning, the tension is critical. You need enough tension to allow you to hold the yarn in place while drafting, but with enough pull so the yarn can feed onto the bobbin.
- The fibres cannot draft.
  Solution: You are letting too much twist into the drafting areas and the fibres cannot move past each other.

As the yarn has a smoother surface than woollen yarn, it may be better for those with sensitive skin. Hats, socks and gloves can also be made from this yarn. Because of its smooth surface, patterns will show up more than with woollen-spun yarn.

Weaving

This is smoother than woollen-spun yarn because the fibres are parallel; therefore it can be used as a warp yarn for blankets and cloth.

■ SPINNING FROM THE FOLD

This is a method I often teach to beginners because it allows good control of the fibres before drafting. It can be used with the short forward or backward draft and combed fibre to produce a yarn very similar to worsted (see photo 3.54).

It is not easy to spin this way using carded fibre, but you can spin semi-woollen yarn if you use combed fibre and the medium draft or long draw (see photo 3.55).

■ SPINDLE SPINNING

The advantages of a drop spindle are its portability and small size. You can take it anywhere and spin in waiting rooms, guild meetings, wherever and whenever you have a spare minute or two. You may get some funny looks and even odder questions: 'Why are you making string?' is a common one. There are many different types and weights of spindles. We will start with a top-whorl spindle but try others to see which suits you best.

Top-whorl spindle: This is sometimes called a high-whorl spindle. The hook is attached to the top of the shaft near the whorl, the circular piece of wood (see photo 3.56, page 70).

Bottom-whorl spindle: These have a hook at the end of the shaft at the opposite end to the whorl (see photo 3.57, page 70).

If you are spinning a fine yarn, choose a lightweight spindle. For thicker yarn, choose a heavier spindle. I didn't know this when I first tried spinning on a spindle, and used a heavy spindle to try to spin fine yarn. The yarn kept breaking, the spindle would drop to the floor, and I would get increasingly frustrated. A good weight to begin with is 40–60gm (1.5–2.2oz).

The spindle should be well balanced. Test drive it by giving it a few twirls before you start spinning. It should revolve quite a few times with just one twirl of the fingers.

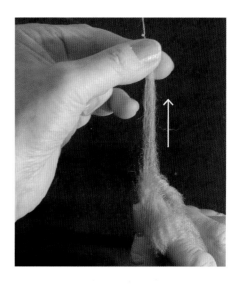

3.54 Fold a short length, about 10–15cm (4–6in) over the forefinger of your back hand. The thumb and second finger control the amount of fibre allowed into the drafting zone by opening and closing.

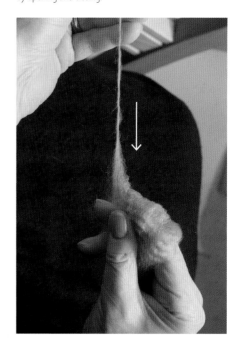

3.55 Draft out from the point of your forefinger. Because you are spinning small amounts at a time, you will need to join the yarn frequently.

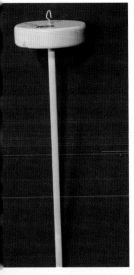

3.58 Tie a 60cm (24in) leader firmly onto the spindle shaft near the whorl with a slip knot as shown, then take the leader over the whorl and through the hook. Tie a loop in the other end of the leader with an overhand knot.

3.59 Practice rotating the spindle until you have a smooth 'twirl'. Hold onto the leader with one hand and rotate the spindle with the other hand by giving the shaft a strong twist clockwise. It is a flicking movement with your thumb and forefinger.

3.60 The fibre should be well prepared so it flows smoothly. The sliver should be broken into narrow strips about 30cm (12in) long. Wrap this length around your wrist to keep it out of the way. Put the thinned-out end of the sliver through the loop in the leader with one hand, your upper hand, making a second loop joining the fibre to the leader. Spin the spindle clockwise with the other (lower) hand.

3.62 After the lower hand has drafted some fibre, the top hand pinches so no more fibre can move into the drafting zone, as the lower hand slides back up, allowing the twist to run into the drafted fibres.

3.56 (above top) Top-whorl spindle.

3.57 (above) Bottom-whorl spindle.

3.61 When the folded fibre begins to twist, the lower hand gently pulls a little of the fibre from the fibre supply in the upper hand (drafting). As the spindle begins to slow, give it another twirl with the lower hand to keep the twist running into the yarn. The lower hand has to do two actions, luckily not at the same time. It has to rotate the spindle and draft. The upper hand just controls the fibre supply. Practise exchanging the right and left hands to see which is easier.

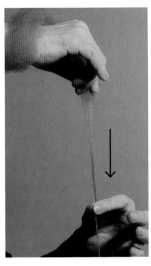
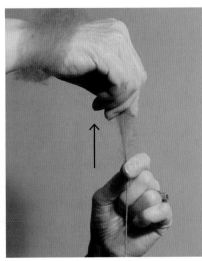

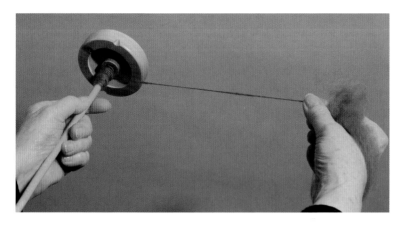

3.63 Winding on. Pinch the yarn where the twist meets the unspun fibre with your upper hand. Unhook the yarn and take the spindle in the other hand with the spun yarn between the spindle and the upper hand. Keep the yarn under tension and wind the yarn firmly around the spindle shaft, also in a clockwise direction, until there is about 20cm (8in) of spun yarn left. Attach this to the hook and begin again.

As with spinning on a wheel, if the drafting is done before the fibre has some twist in it, the yarn will break. The spindle then falls to the floor. Join on new fibre by holding some thin, fluffy fibres against the spun yarn and start again. Keep spinning until the spun yarn is about 1m (1yd) long. If you are standing up and have long arms you may be able to spin a longer length. When the spindle shaft is full of yarn it will become heavy and unbalanced so stop before this point. Wind the yarn off the spindle into a ball, and fill the spindle again. When you have two balls, place them in containers and ply. For a beginner it is best to ply from the two balls. More experienced spinners can ply from one centre-pull ball.

PLYING

The action is almost the same as spinning but in this case the spindle is rotated anticlockwise.

SKEINING

Skein the yarn off the spindle. Stand the spindle on the floor, wedged between your feet, and wind it onto the niddy noddy. Follow the washing instructions on pages 31–32.

◼ CONCLUSION

After reading through this chapter you can see why I said there is no limit to the range of yarns you can spin. By changing the preparation, the way this prepared fibre is split before spinning, and the spinning method itself, you can spin any type of yarn for a myriad of different uses.

Add to this the information in later chapters about the different fibres you can choose, and there is enough variation to keep you busy experimenting for several lifetimes. In nearly 50 years, I have not become proficient in all aspects of spinning. But I am still having fun learning.

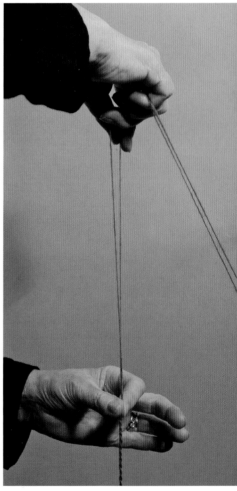

3.64 Plying on a spindle. Hold the two singles in the upper hand and draft down with the lower hand. Check you have enough twist and don't fill the spindle too full.

PROJECTS

Many of the yarns described in this chapter can be used for embroidery. They can be spun to suit any requirements, e.g., the yarn can be textured or smooth, dull or shiny, thick or thin. For this cross-stitch embroidery thread, the yarn was fine and smooth, allowing the individual threads to clearly show the crosses.

Embroidered cross-stitch

Using spindle-spun merino wool by Gail Russell

3.65 Embroidered cross-stitch.

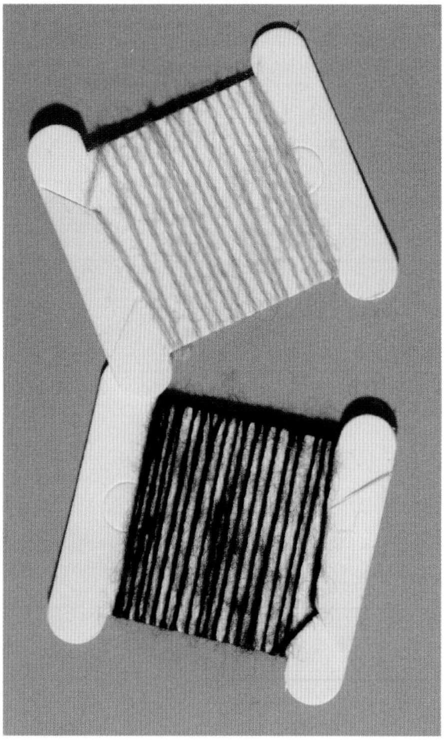

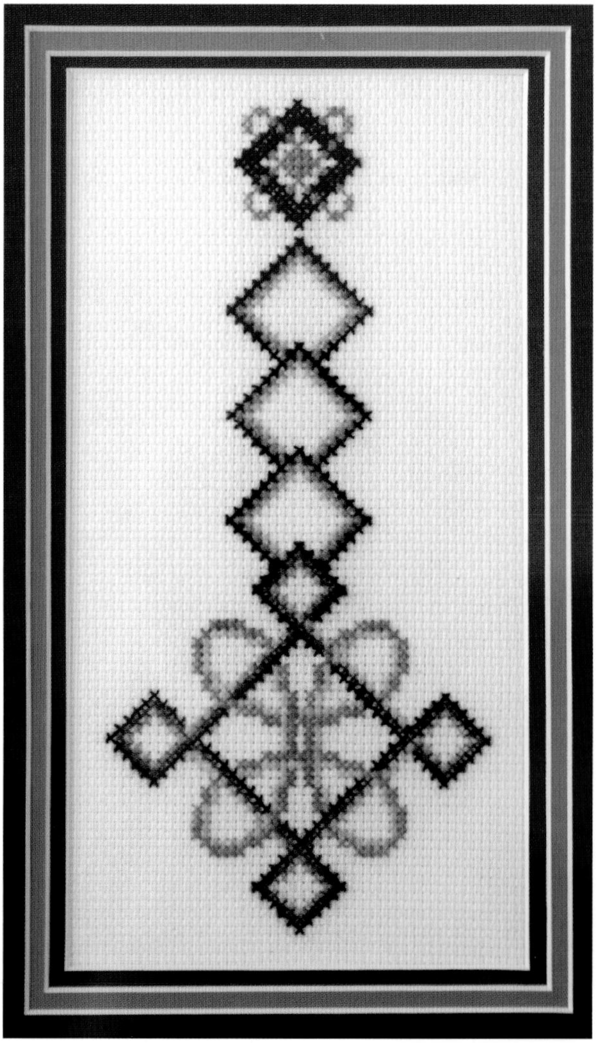

Woven worsted-spun fabric
by Anne Field

Worsted-spun yarn such as this is suitable for weaving (or knitting) into skirt, jacket or coat fabric as it is hard-wearing, will not pill or sag and drapes well. I bought this Romney top randomly dyed in shades of blue. I spun it worsted to make a firm, smooth yarn for both warp and weft. There were 22 wraps per 2.5cm (1in) in the finished, washed two-ply yarn. Because it was spun worsted, it resisted abrasion in the heddles and reed.

My first weaving using handspun yarns was a disaster. The yarn was too thick and I beat too heavily so the fabric was inflexible and solid when it was cut off the loom. Since then I have learnt to weave a more open fabric as I now know that handspun wool is very hard-wearing and doesn't need heavy beating to make it long-lasting.

3.66 Fibre and skein of yarn used for woven worsted-spun fabric.

I used the niddy noddy to measure the yarn and determined that 500g (18oz) measured 1650m (1790yd). A good guide when working out how much yarn you need for warp and weft is to allow two-thirds of the warp weight for the weft. The total amount of handspun weighed 500g (18oz), therefore I allowed 300g (10.8oz) for the warp and 200g (7.2oz) for the weft.

Structure: Broken twill, woven in 2/2 twill
Equipment: 4-shaft loom, 77cm (30in) wide, one shuttle, 12 dent reed
Warp and weft yarn: 500g (18oz) handspun wool, worsted-spun
Warp length: 2.8m (3yd); 336 ends
Width in reed: 71cm (28in)
Sett: 12 ends per 2.5cm (1in). 1 per dent in 12 dent reed
Picks per 2.5cm (1in): 12
Weight of finished fabric: 434g (15.2oz)

Weaving

Weave in 2/2 twill for the warp length. I hemstitched both ends. I handwashed the fabric in warm soapy water, rinsed it, and dried it lying flat. Press while slightly damp.

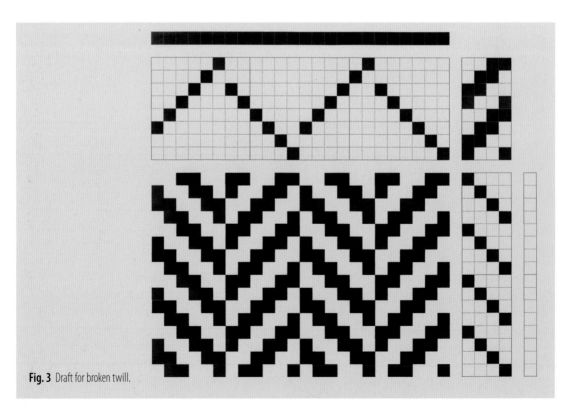

Fig. 3 Draft for broken twill.

Woollen hat
Knitted by Anne Field

I spun the wool for this hat from a carded Romney fleece. The wool measured 10 wraps per 2.5cm (1in), and I used size 5.5mm (US 8, UK 5) needles.

Adult's basic hat pattern from Sandra Dain

This basic hat pattern can be knitted in many ways.

Use 4.5mm (US 6, UK 7) needles and double-weight yarn, or 4mm (US 5, UK 8) needles if the yarn is finer. Straight or circular needles.

Cast on between 100 and 110 sts and work 24–26 rows of rib (K1, P1, or K2, P2). Or work 10–12 rows for a beanie (100 sts is for an average-size head).

Change to stocking stitch and work about 26–30 rows. After about 6 rows of stocking stitch, you can work in a contrast — stripes, Fair Isle or motifs.

Begin decreasing. If you have a number of sts that won't divide by 10 (e.g., 105), work a row to get rid of these excess stitches, or 2 rows if you are not knitting the hat on circular needles. Then work as follows:

Row 1: K8, K2 tog. Repeat to end of row.
Row 2: P.
Row 3: K7, K2 tog. Repeat to end of row.
Row 4: P.

Continue as above, working 1 st fewer on the decrease row each time until nearly all the sts are worked off (about 6–8 will remain). Break off the yarn and run a thread through these sts. Fasten off securely.

3.67 Knitted, woollen-spun hat.

Sew up the side seam. Another style, which I used for the hat in the photograph above, is to begin with stocking stitch, omitting the rib altogether. After about 12 rows you can do 6 rows of reversed stocking stitch. This makes a firm edge for the hat. Keep knitting until it is time to do the decreases. This will produce a rolled-up-brim type of hat.

A child's hat (11.2, page 175) can be made in a similar way, using fewer sts. The hat can be worked using a 40cm circular needle, i.e., all knit, no purling and little sewing up. When about 60 sts remain, the circular needle will need to be replaced by a set of 4 needles.

Feather & fan shawl/scarf
Spun by Anne Field
Designed & knitted by Mary-Anne Mace

I spun this wool from 200g (8oz) of hand-dyed merino roving from the supplier Scarlet Fleece, USA. I spun the yarn worsted as I wanted the pattern to show up clearly. The size was 18 wraps to 2.5cm (1in).

Pattern notes

This shawl is shaped like a shallow, elongated triangle. This is achieved by increasing twice the number of stitches at the garter edges of the shawl compared to the spine of the shawl, which has increases only on the right side (the edges have increases on both right and wrong sides of the shawl). When the stockinette section is completed, there are no more increases at the spine, yet increases continue on both right and wrong sides at the garter edges. The feather-and-fan border is centrally placed in such a way that a section of yarn overs, that create the feather-and-fan pattern, appears to continue the spine of the shawl. Odd rows are the right side, even rows the wrong side.

Abbreviations

pm = place marker. These markers are slipped when you come to them. They mark the 2 garter-edge sts at each end of the shawl, and the centre stitch at the spine of the shawl.

yo = yarn over (creating a stitch by wrapping yarn around the needle)

RS = right-side row

WS = wrong-side row

kf&b (or k front and back) = knit into the stitch knitwise, and without slipping it off the needle, knit into the back loop of the same stitch and slip the 2 sts off together. You have created an extra stitch.

Beginning tab

With 4mm (US 5, UK 8) circular needles (100cm long):

Cast on 2 sts.

Knit 6 rows.

Row 7: Knit these 2 sts and carry on and knit 3 sts in the garter ridges along the long edge of the tab you have just made, knit 2 sts in cast-on edge — 7 sts in total.

Main shawl
Stocking-stitch section

Row 1: K2, pm, yo, K1, yo, pm, K1, pm, yo, K1, yo, pm, K2 (11 sts).

Row 2: K2, yo, P7, yo, K2 (13 sts).

Row 3: K2, yo, K4, yo, K1, yo, K4, yo, K2 (17 sts).

3.68 Feather-and-fan shawl/scarf.

Row 4: K2, yo, p across to last st marker, yo, K2 (19 sts).

Row 5: K2, yo, K to 2nd marker, yo, K1, yo, K to last marker, yo, K2 (23 sts).

Continue in this way, repeating row 4 and 5, increasing by 2 sts every WS row and 4 sts every RS row until you have 239 sts on the needle and ending on a RS row.

Feather-and-fan border

With WS facing, you now increase as usual (yo) in the space adjacent to the 2 garter-edge sts on both sides, except there are *no more increases* at the spine. The feather-and-fan pattern follows:

Row 1: (WS) K2, yo, knit to last 2 sts, yo, K2.

Row 2: (RS) K2, yo, knit to last 2 sts, yo, K2.

Row 3: (WS) K2, yo, purl to last 2 sts, yo, K2.

Row 4: (RS) K2, yo, K4, *(K2tog) 3 times, (yo, K1) 6 times, (K2 tog) 3 times*, repeat from * to * to last 5 sts, K2, kf&b, yo, K2. (The k front and back is to make an extra stitch to have sufficient stitches for the feather-and-fan pattern and is only done this one time. (248 sts).

Row 5–7: Repeat rows 1–3.

Row 8: K2, yo, K8, *(K2tog) 3 times, (yo, K1) 6 times, (K2tog) 3 times*, repeat from * to * to last 10 sts, K8, yo, K2.

Row 9–11: Repeat rows 1–3.

Row 12: K2, yo, K12, *(K2tog) 3 times, (yo, K1) 6 times, (K2tog) 3 times*, repeat from * to * to last 14 sts, K12, yo, K2.

Rows 13–15: Repeat rows 1–3.

Row 16: K2, yo, K16, *(K2tog) 3 times, (yo, K1) 6 times, (K2tog) 3 times*, repeat from * to * to last 18 sts, K16, yo, K2.

Row 17–19: repeat rows 1–3.

Row 20: K2, yo, K2, *(K2tog) 3 times, (yo, K1) 6 times, (K2tog) 3 times*, repeat from * to * to last 4 sts, K2, yo, K2.

Row 21–23: Repeat rows 1–3.

Row 24: K2, yo, K6, *(K2tog) 3 times, (yo, K1) 6 times, (K2tog) 3 times*, repeat from * to * to last 8 sts, K6, yo, K2.

Row 25–27: Repeat rows 1–3.

Row 28: K2, yo, K10, *(K2tog) 3 times, (yo, K1) 6 times, (K2tog) 3 times*, repeat from * to * to last 12 sts, K10, yo, K2.

Rows 29–31: Repeat rows 1–3.

Row 32: K2, yo, K14, *(K2tog) 3 times, (yo, K1) 6 times, (K2tog) 3 times*, repeat from * to * to last 16 sts, K14, yo, K2.

Rows 33–35: Repeat rows 1–3.

Row 36: K2, yo, *(K2tog) 3 times, (yo, K1) 6 times, (K2tog) 3 times*, repeat from * to * to last 2 sts, yo, K2.

Rows 37–39: Repeat rows 1–3.

Row 40: K2, yo, K4, *(K2tog) 3 times, (yo, K1) 6 times, (K2tog) 3 times*, repeat from * to * to last 6 sts, K4, yo, K2.

Row 41: K2, yo, knit to last 2 sts, yo, K2.

Row 42: K2, yo, knit to last 2 sts, yo, K2.

Cast off knitwise *very loosely* with wrong side facing.

This shawl can easily be made bigger by continuing the pattern as established after row 40. You just continue adding 4 knit sts at either end of the shawl each 4th row until you have at least 18 sts for a new feather-and-fan repeat. In this case, row 44 would be the same as row 8. Alternatively you could add more rows to the stocking-stitch section. This would be a little more tricky because you would have to work out how many plain knit stitches you would have to do before starting the feather-and-fan repeat in order to get the yarn over section of the feather-and-fan pattern centred correctly at the spine of the shawl.

3.69 Skein of yarn and roving.

SOURCES

Dyed Romney top for woven-fabric project, from Elspeth Wilkinson, Wool, Yarn & Fibres, Christchurch, New Zealand.

Tai Tapu Wool Carders: green-acres@hotmail.com

Merino hand-dyed wool roving for knitted shawl/scarf from Scarlet Fleece, US: www.ScarletFleece.com

Part Two
ANIMAL FIBRES

II Animal fibres

WOOL HAS ALWAYS been the most common and popular fibre for spinners and beginner spinners find it the easiest to start with. It is widely available, it flows well because of the wool scales, and it comes in many colours, from white to dark brown. Every country has its own breeds of sheep and spinners soon learn which are their favourites. The variety in sheep breeds means that they can be spun into a wide range of articles, from fine shawls to upholstery fabric. Chapter 4 describes how to spin this valuable fibre.

I spun only wool for the first 30 years so I found spinning other fibres a big leap. As I became more adventurous, I wanted to spin alpaca, silk and mohair but didn't quite know where to start. What projects were they suitable for? How should I prepare and spin them? However, I found that the transition from wool to spinning other protein fibres was actually easier than I had envisaged.

Over the years I have handled hundreds of sheep-wool fleeces from around the world and so have developed a sound knowledge and background for making decisions about quality and what each breed is suitable for. I can look at the crimp, length of fibre, and decide how fine to spin the yarn, but I had to find different ways to learn about and assess fibres other than wool.

I am basically a self-taught spinner and weaver: I learn by doing. So I decided a good method of working out how to spin these other fibres was to look at the fibre in its raw state to find out its characteristics. Then I would prepare and spin the yarn to enhance the fibre. This meant I was working *with* each fibre, not *against* it, which is easier to do than to try to change the fibre properties. As I became more confident, I found I could change the characteristics of the raw material: for example, I could take a soft, fluffy fibre and spin it into a smooth, solid yarn suitable for weaving.

In the next few chapters we will do just that. First we will look at the characteristics of each fibre, then spin a yarn that echoes those qualities. Then we will look at other methods of preparation and spinning to make different yarns.

You can learn so much just by putting your hands into a bag of fibre. Is it soft, prickly or springy? Hold the fibres up to the light. How are they prepared? Are the fibres parallel or messed up? Hold a group of fibres in your hands and try to pull them apart. Are they strong or weak? Are they elastic?

Of course each animal fibre will have different characteristics, but as we work with small amounts at a time, and usually from just one animal, unlike industrial processors of animal fibres, we can learn most of what we need to know by looking and touching the raw material.

If you are spinning a fibre that is new to you, sample skeins, spun, plied and washed, will give you plenty of valuable information. You can measure the skein before and after washing to measure the shrinkage. You can also see if the fibre blooms and expands with washing, and whether it becomes dull or shiny.

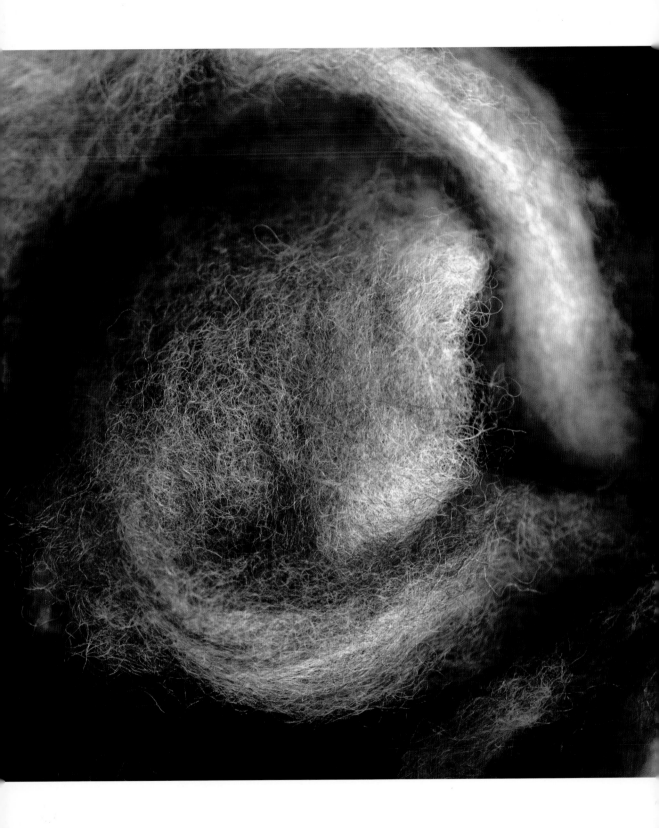

Wool

4.1 Shearing a sheep (Stuart Albrey).

WOOL BASICS

WE TOUCHED BRIEFLY on the subject of wool in the first chapter, just enough to get you started, but in this chapter we will look at this fibre in detail.

Wool is a renewable resource. Sheep need to get rid of their fleeces periodically because the wool load can become heavy and matted if it is left on for too long. One famous sheep, called Shrek, was not shorn for six years and had a fleece which weighed 31kg (68lb) with a staple length of 27cm (10½in). I saw a sample of his fleece and it was amazingly long and clean. However, most sheep, if left unshorn, will suffer, especially in the heat. They can also become so heavy that they become cast and cannot get up.

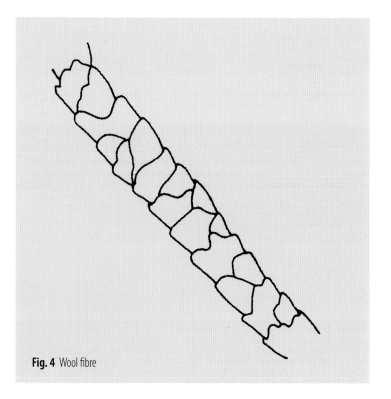

Fig. 4 Wool fibre

CHARACTERISTICS OF WOOL

- Wool is a poor conductor of heat, which keeps in body warmth, and it generates heat when it absorbs water vapour from the air. Yet it is also water-resistant.
- It does not hold static electricity.
- It will burn in but not out of the flame, leaving a black, crushable bead, and is therefore more fire resistant than many other fibres.
- It dyes well.
- It is elastic, particularly the fine-wool breeds, which have plenty of crimp — the natural waves in wool.
- It is a useful fibre to blend with others, such as alpaca or silk.
- It contains grease.

Primitive sheep were double-coated, with a coarse, hairy outer coat and a soft undercoat. As it was the undercoat which was preferred for clothing, gradually sheep were bred without the outer, coarse layer, although some primitive breeds still exist today. Before the advent of shears to remove the fleece, sheep shed their wool when it became too long. I have seen sheep in the process of shedding their wool, and I was interested to see how matted and unkempt this wool was.

A severe drought in my home province of Canterbury one year caused this shedding and the resultant fleeces were unusable. It was a sorry sight to see.

Now we remove fleeces by shearing. In New Zealand we usually shear at the end of winter before lambing. One of the reasons for this is that the ewe will feel the cold more and move into shelter to have her lambs, thus protecting them from the cold. Also any break in the wool, caused by a difficult lambing, is minimised.

Wool is an interesting protein fibre. Each fibre grows out of a follicle in the skin. A fine breed, such as merino, may have more than 60,000 fibres. The main part of the fibre is the cortex, which is surrounded by a thin outer layer called the cuticle. The cuticle consists of a layer of overlapping scales which point towards the tip of the fibre. It is these scales that make wool an easy fibre to spin because they catch on each other during the drafting process and help to pull out adjacent fibres. The grease in wool, which protects the fibres, also lubricates them (and you!) if you spin with unwashed fleece.

Merino

Polwarth

Half-bred Hampshire Down

Perendale

Texel

Romney

Gotland

Coopworth

English Leicester

Borderdale

Lincoln

Drysdale

4.2 Fleece sample with named breeds.

MICRONS

Wool is classified for fineness by measuring it in microns. A micron is one-millionth of a metre; therefore the lower the number, the finer the wool. Fine wools also have more crimps to the centimetre (or inch) than coarser wools, making them more elastic, and they are usually shorter in staple length.

ENHANCING THE QUALITIES OF WOOL

Because wool is such a long-standing and valuable fibre, there have been many advances made to enhance its qualities.

Optim™

This is a technology developed by the CSIRO in Australia which takes merino wool and radically changes the wool fibre, structure and properties. The fibres are softer, stronger and lighter than the untreated wool. The process stretches 19 micron fibres between 40–50%, reducing the micron count by 3–3.5 microns. This reduction is then chemically set. These treated fibres can also be blended with normal wool.

Shrink-proofing wool

This is also done with merino and spinners can buy shrink-proofed tops to spin. When washed the yarn will not shrink or felt. This can be a great advantage with garments that require a lot of washing, such as baby wear.

There are various processes that can be used: one involves using a chlorine agent, another coats the fibres with a resin, and another can process the wool so the scales do not catch on each other and cause felting and shrinking.

When spinning these tops, the fibres become more slippery and may need more twist to keep the yarn together.

■ SHEEP BREEDS

It is always surprising to new spinners just how many different breeds of sheep there are in the world. Each breed has its own characteristics and it is worthwhile learning what is the best breed for your particular needs.

When I was spinning yarn for jerseys for my children, I chose Romney fleeces, not only because they were easy to spin, but because they produced hard-wearing outdoor garments. If you want to spin very fine yarn for a lacy shawl, you would choose a fine-wool sheep breed such as Corriedale or merino.

I cannot hope to tell you about all the breeds in this book, so in the Further Reading section at the end of this book, I have listed some books which will give you more detail about the different breeds. However, the following sheep breeds are some favourites of spinners.

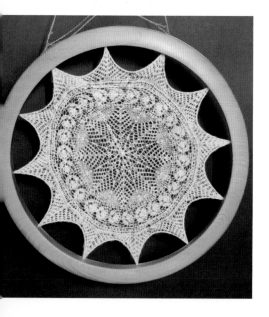

4.3 Lace posy by Margaret Stove. Worsted-spun and knitted from a merino fleece.

4.4 Merino ram (Stuart Albrey).

MERINO
Micron count: 14–24
Average staple length: 7.5cm (3in)

Characteristics

A fine, closely crimped wool. With a white fleece, the colour is definitely white, not creamy, with little lustre and a flat tip to the staple. It is not as hard-wearing as other wool, will felt easily and has a high grease content, which makes washing before spinning the usual practice. Wash small amounts carefully, soaking in hot, soapy water without any agitation as this will cause felting, then rinse. I have used mesh bags or mesh plastic trays, as I can then lift the trays or bags out of the water without agitating or disturbing the staple formation.

Spinning

As it is a short fibre it may be difficult to flick-card and comb and is usually prepared by pulling off the tips by hand, as these may be weak and cause pilling in the finished garment. Then the wool is hand- or drum-carded. However, I have seen long-staple merino fleeces which can be flick-carded or combed so check the staple length first.

It can be spun worsted, semi-worsted, woollen or semi-woollen. It is best spun into a fine yarn with a high twist and used for garments that will not require constant washing, as they will felt. It will increase in size considerably when the finished yarn is washed and will be very springy and bouncy. Beginners may need more experience before tackling this fibre.

Uses

It is not hard-wearing, so shawls and scarves are ideally suited to the soft handle of this yarn. Too much washing will cause felting.

Washing tip

At one workshop I taught, a student told us about washing portions of her fleece in cat litter trays. Everyone rushed to the nearest pet shop, to the surprise of the shop assistants. One solid tray held the water; the other perforated tray held the staples and fitted inside the water tray. So you just lifted the inside tray out when the staples had soaked enough.

4.5a Polwarth sheep (Wendy Dennis).
4.5b Polwarth sheep in yard.

POLWARTH
Micron count: 21–26
Average staple length:10cm (4in)

Characteristics
Polwarth is three-quarters merino and a quarter Lincoln, so it has many of the characteristics of merino. The Lincoln content gives slightly more lustre and length to the fleece, but it is still very soft. Polwarth was the first Australian breed and was bred by Alexander Dennis in 1880 from his farm Tarndwarncoort. If it has a high grease content, wash as for merino.

Spinning

Because of its length, it can usually be flick-carded or combed for worsted or semi-woollen spinning, or hand- or drum-carded for woollen and semi-worsted spinning. It will increase in size when washed because of the high merino content and has a springy, bouncy feel to the yarn.

Uses
Use for scarves and shawls, and also for fine lacy knitwear.

4.6 Corriedale sheep (Tai Tapu Wool Carders).

CORRIEDALE

Micron count: 26–33
Average staple length: 10cm (4in)

Characteristics

This is a breed of half merino and half Lincoln or English Leicester sheep. As the merino genes are less than in the Polwarth, this fleece is more lustrous and longer in staple length. It is a very popular breed among spinners and is a good choice for beginners.

Spinning

It can be spun worsted, semi-worsted, woollen or semi-woollen. It will increase in size with washing but not as much as merino or Polwarth.

Uses

Use for scarves and shawls, also for garments, such as jerseys, hats, gloves and mittens, and blankets.

4.7 Romney sheep and lamb (Stuart Albrey).

ROMNEY
Micron Count: 31–38
Average staple length: 15cm (6in)

Characteristics
This is the most common sheep in New Zealand and is an excellent breed for beginners to start with. The staple has a pointed tip, and its length makes it an easy fibre to spin. It is lustrous and, when the fleece is white, it is creamy in colour.

Spinning

The finished yarn won't change much in size when washed. It is ideal for worsted and semi-woollen yarn, but may be too long to hand- or drum-card.

Uses
It makes hard-wearing woven cloth for outer wear, skirts and jackets. Knit outdoor, hard-wearing jerseys, hats, gloves and socks.

ENGLISH LEICESTER

Micron count: 37–40
Average staple length: 18cm (7in)

Characteristics

This is a strong, long stapled fleece with a high lustre.

Spinning

Spin into a medium to coarse yarn with a low twist to make this yarn soft. If spun fine with lots of twist, it will be stringy and harsh. It is too long to card so can be flick-carded or combed. The finished yarn will not change with washing.

Uses

It is ideal for a warp yarn and makes excellent upholstery fabric. It is usually too harsh for knitted jerseys but can be knitted into outer wear such as jackets and coats. I have frequently used it for woven-fleece floor rugs in its raw, washed state as it has a curly tip which gives the finished rug an interesting texture.

DOWN BREEDS

Average micron count: 23–32
Average staple length: 5–8cm (2–3in)

Characteristics

Down breeds include Dorset Down, Hampshire Down, Suffolk, Shropshire and Southdown. Cheviot is also included in this range.

These sheep are primarily bred for their meat rather than wool, so their fleeces aren't used as much by spinners as the previous breeds. The wool is usually short and very crimpy, with a high degree of elasticity. Beginner spinners will not find this type of wool easy to spin because it is so short and elastic. The wool has a very spongy feel and will increase markedly with washing. It doesn't felt easily.

Spinning

Usually these fleeces are too short for flick-carding or combing but can be hand- or drum-carded for woollen or semi-worsted yarn.

Uses

Because of the very spongy nature of this wool, it makes excellent socks and blankets.

4.8 English Leicester ewe and lamb (Geoff Bryant).

4.9 Suffolk ewe with her triplets (Geoff Bryant).

Sheep coats

Many sheep farmers now put coats on their sheep to protect the wool, especially in cold climates where the sheep must spend part of the year in barns. This helps prevent the wool from getting weathered or bleached at the tips.

■ BLACK & COLOURED SHEEP

When I first started spinning, any sheep that weren't white were quickly dispatched to the meatworks. All the manufacturers wanted white fleece, with no coloured fibres to contaminate the wool as this affected the dye colours. However, now spinners value the wide range of natural colours, and many black and coloured flocks are bred especially for spinners. The colours range from a pale silver grey to a dark brown. Moorit, a red brown, is another colour beloved by spinners and can be found in many breeds. Pale grey and brown fleeces can be overdyed to give more subtle colours than a white fleece.

Coloured fleeces also usually have a variation of colour within one fleece, and many spinners use this to their advantage to make randomly striped garments. The fleece can be sorted first so colour changes can be planned or the wool can be blended on hand or drum carders for a more uniform colour.

The sun and the weather can bleach the tips of black and coloured fleeces, and this can add to their distinctive appearance, but check that these tips are not weak. If they pull off easily, they will break off and cause pilling in the finished garment. I once sent off a beautiful moorit lamb's fleece to be carded, and it came back with all the broken, weak tips in the batts, making it unsuitable for spinning. These weak tips can be cut off before carding. Flick-carding and combing will remove these tips, but hand- and drum-carding leaves them in the wool. Lamb's fleeces are usually tippy.

4.10 Black and coloured sheep (Ironwater Ranch, USA).

▨ SORTING A FLEECE

Fleeces need to be skirted; that is, the dirty, hairy wool that is not up to the standard of the rest of the fleece is removed. On the farm, this is usually done immediately after shearing. Each fleece is laid out on a slatted table, tips uppermost, to be skirted. When I lived in an area of New Zealand with a high rainfall, most of the wool from the centre of the sheep's back would be removed as this would have had the protective grease washed out, and the wool would be weak and tender. Skirting also removes the wool that is matted and stained and contains lots of vegetable matter and second cuts. These are very short pieces caused by the shearer making a second pass.

If you have to skirt the fleece yourself, you will lose the portion of it that is discarded, so make sure you pay less for an unskirted fleece. Most sellers who supply wool to spinners will have carefully done this work for you, and I expect to pay more for this type of fleece. But do check the condition of a fleece before you buy. I once tipped a bag of fleece out onto the shop floor to find the dirty wool all tucked neatly in at the bottom of the bag.

As well as removing the soiled and obviously damaged wool, you should also remove any wool that has a different crimp count to the

4.11 Fleece on skirting table after shearing.

4.12 Skirted fleece. The second cuts fall through the slats in the table.

4.13 Removing a staple of wool from a fleece.

rest of the fleece. Crimp is the wave in the staple. Wool with a high crimp with close-set waves is finer and more elastic than wool with a widely spaced crimp pattern. Mixing these two types of staples will cause the spun yarn to vary in elasticity and style.

When you take a staple of wool from a fleece, don't tug it to remove it as this disturbs the rest of the surrounding fleece. Hold the staple with the forefinger and thumb of one hand while placing the forefinger and thumb of the other hand around the base of the staple. Firmly pull out the staple while preventing any more wool following it with the other hand. This way you get a clear, well-defined staple for combing or carding.

CHOOSING A FLEECE

- Unless you've opted for an unskirted fleece, it should be clean and free of vegetable matter.
- Check for soundness. Take a staple between your two hands and give it a sharp tug. It should 'ping'. A break in a staple indicates a weak area that may be caused by lack of feed, drought or a difficult lamb birth. It is hard to see a break by holding a staple up to the light, so do the 'ping' test.
- Is it well skirted?
- Any stains should be able to be washed out. You can test for this by washing a staple or two.
- The crimp should be even over the staple length and over most of the fleece. This means the elasticity will be consistent.
- There should be no second cuts.
- Check that the staple tips are strong. Test this by trying to strip the tip off with your fingers. If too much of the tip breaks off, discard this fleece.

WASHING A FLEECE

Some spinners will not spin unwashed wool; others like the feel of the grease as they spin. I prefer to spin worsted yarn from greasy, clean wool, but for woollen spinning I like to wash the wool first. However, I have a wide range of good, clean fleeces to choose from in New Zealand and other spinners may not be so lucky. If you are storing wool for a while, it is advisable to wash it first as the grease will harden and make the wool difficult to spin later. Most fleeces will lose about a quarter of their weight when washed. Washing a fleece before spinning also gives a true indication of its colour. Once I bought a fleece I thought was pale grey, only to find it was white when I washed it.

Most spinners have their own favourite way to wash their wool, but here are some helpful hints:

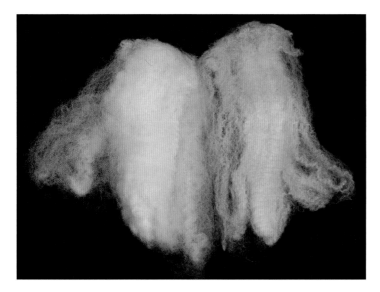

4.14 Washed and unwashed staples.

4.15 (below) Storing fleeces.

- The greasier the wool, the hotter the water should be. See the tip on page 89 for washing merino as this is a wool with a high grease content.
- Do not wash a complete fleece in one session. That will almost guarantee the weather will turn nasty and you will be left with piles of sodden, smelly wool.
- Chose a warm, sunny, windy day and work on a small portion at a time.
- Plastic mesh baskets that will fit into your laundry tub are ideal. This means you will not be agitating the wool, as this can cause felting.
- If the wool is very dirty, I soak it in cold water, in the mesh basket, for an hour or two at a time, changing the water two or three times. When you change the water, lift the basket up, push down on the wool to remove the excess water, let the dirty water run away, then refill the tub and immerse the basket again.
- Fill the tub with hot, soapy water, using a mild laundry detergent, immerse the basket of wool and let it soak for a few minutes. You can also buy special wool-wash detergents.
- Lift the basket out and push down to remove the excess water as before.
- If the wool is still very dirty, you may need to repeat the hot, soapy wash again.
- Rinse in warm water.
- To hasten the drying, you can put the wool into bags (I use old pillow cases) in the washing machine to spin out the excess water. Don't put it in the washing machine unbagged. A friend did this once — the wool clogged the machine and the repair was costly.
- Put the wool outside on a slatted table in the sun to dry. Wool yellows in sunlight so do not leave it out for days. Never use a tumble drier.

Storing a fleece

Don't use plastic bags as the wool can sweat inside these. Use calico bags, plastic storage bins or cardboard boxes. If you have a moth problem, use plastic storage bins with tight lids. You can also see what is inside these bins, which is an advantage. It is helpful to leave a record with the stored fleeces, naming the breed, source and date acquired. Do not store damp wool as it can go mouldy.

■ **PROJECT**

Jacket
Spun & knitted in Romney wool by Ann Smillie

This knitted jacket was originally designed by Deryn Pittar from New Zealand and printed in the *Web Magazine*, June 1980. It resurfaced in the booklet *Patterns from the Web: Requested Favourites*. So you can see it has been a long-standing favourite. It is reproduced here with permission.

Needle size: 8mm (US 11, UK 0)
Wool: Romney fleece, already carded and dyed. 10 wraps per 2.5cm (1in), 230gm (8oz).
Note: Panels of 12 rows are knitted in pattern. All other rows refer to garter stitch, i.e., 3, 6, 10, 20. Back and front are knitted across, left to right or vice versa. Sleeves are knitted downwards.

Pattern (© Deryn Pittar)

Row 1: K3, * K2tog, wool forward *, repeat from * to * to last 10 sts, K10.

Row 2: K9, * K2tog, wool forward *, repeat from * to * to last 4 sts, K4.

This gives a lacy hole effect. To set holes on panels, an even number of stitches (70) is used and the pattern rows become:

Row 1: K4, pattern to last 10 sts, K10.

Row 2: K10, pattern to last 4 sts, K4.

Back: Cast on 69 sts.

Fronts (do two): Cast on 69 sts.

Sleeves (do two): Cast on 39 sts. Keep 4 sts garter-stitch border at each edge of pattern i.e., K3, pattern to last 4 sts, K4. Repeat for each row.

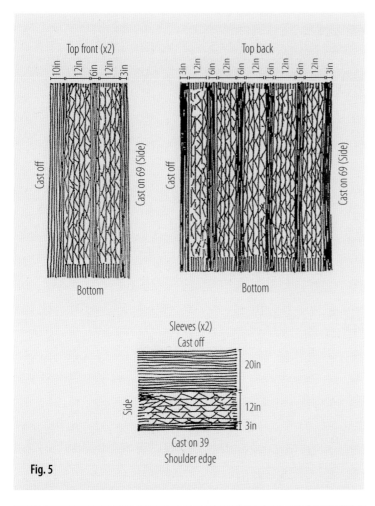

Top front (x2)

10in 12in 6in 12in 3in

Cast off

Cast on 69 (Side)

Bottom

Top back

3in 12in 6in 12in 6in 12in 6in 12in 6in 12in 3in

Cast off

Cast on 69 (Side)

Bottom

Sleeves (x2)
Cast off

20in

Side

12in

3in

Cast on 39
Shoulder edge

Fig. 5

To make up

Join shoulder seams, front to back. Join sleeves to shoulder, firm edge. Join sides up and underarm sleeve seam. No neck shaping is needed as it sits well. Sleeves can be omitted for drop-shoulder effect. They can also be knitted wider (say 59 sts) and longer to three-quarter length or full length. Pockets or a knitted belt can be added. Once you have tried this, the variations are endless.

SOURCES

There are many places to buy wool, from farms to shops.
There are lists of wool suppliers in the *Spin-Off* magazine by Interweave Press:
www.interweave.com
Most shops that sell spinning wheels also sell wool.
Romney fleeces:
www.ironwater.com,
www.fffnz.com
Polwarth fleeces:
www.tarndwarncoort.com
Merino fleeces: www.fffnz.com
Corriedale fleeces:
greenacres@ hotmail.com

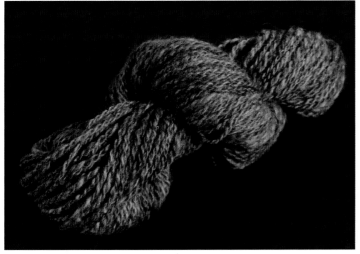

4.16 Skein of wool used to make the jacket on the opposite page.

Alpaca

5

ALPACAS ARE PART of the camelid family, which includes the camel, llama, vicuna and guanaco. All these animals have fibre that can be spun, but alpacas in particular have become very popular in the last few years for spinners. There are two types of alpaca: huacaya and suri. These are not separate breeds, but rather different fibre types.

Alpacas are single-coated, unlike llamas and camels, which have a long, strong outer coat and a soft inner coat. It is the soft undercoat which is prized by spinners, so when spinning camel or llama, the outer coat has to be separated first. This single coat of the alpaca makes it quick and easy to prepare.

Alpacas are native to South America but have spread across much of the rest of the world. It is quite common to see these animals grazing in New Zealand paddocks and it always surprises me that these exotic-looking animals seem so at home here. They are beautiful to look at with their long necks and large lustrous eyes, with eyelashes which would be the envy of any teenage girl. But alpacas pack a nasty spit, unlike most teenage girls I know. There are more than 20 colours of fibre, ranging from white through to black.

Alpacas love to roll in dirt and dust, so their coats are often contaminated, although a good shaking can remove much of the dust. Unlike wool, the fibre contains no grease so dust is more easily removed.

The fibre looks like wool, especially the huacaya fibre, but is termed hair rather than wool as it has a different structure, with a medulla — a central core, which has a series of small air sacs. The scales are flatter than those of a wool fibre, adding to the soft, smooth handle.

5.1 Huacaya alpaca Apollo (above) and Huacaya cria (below) from Highway Star Farm.

5.2 Suri alpaca from Homestead Farm (Anne Rogers).

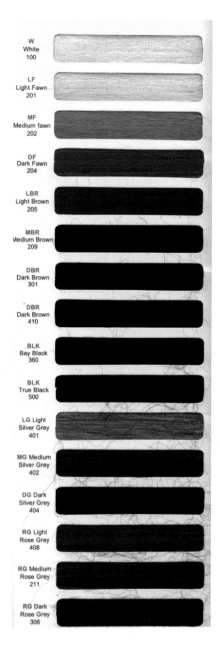

W White 100		
LF Light Fawn 201		
MF Medium fawn 202		
DF Dark Fawn 204		
LBR Light Brown 205		
MBR Medium Brown 209		
DBR Dark Brown 301		
DBR Dark Brown 410		
BLK Bay Black 360		
BLK True Black 500		
LG Light Silver Grey 401		
MG Medium Silver Grey 402		
DG Dark Silver Grey 404		
RG Light Rose Grey 408		
RG Medium Rose Grey 211		
RG Dark Rose Grey 306		

5.3 Alpaca colour range, with kind permission from the New Zealand Alpaca Association.

SHEARING

Most animals are shorn once a year and the fibre length can vary over the same animal. Alpacas are restrained when shorn.

SKIRTING

This may have been done before you acquired the fibre, but still check by spreading out the fibre on a slatted table with the tips uppermost. The best fibre comes from the saddle (or blanket) area. Remove any matted or stained pieces, areas contaminated with vegetable matter and any fibres that are different in appearance from the bulk of the fibre. These will be short, hairy fibres which will have come from the legs and belly.

Check for a break in the fibres by pulling out several staples from different sections and pull each staple apart with a swift tug. These weakened areas are caused by stress, such as from weaning. If there is any break or tenderness it may show up as a dip in the crimp structure. If so, discard that portion. Fibre from a cria (first-year) fleece may have a weakened tip, but this can be cut or pulled off if the staples that are left are long enough to spin. You should be left with fibre that is the same length and similar in appearance.

Store the skirted blankets in calico bags, or plastic, lidded containers, not plastic bags. It is a good idea to label the fibre with the source, date bought and any other useful information.

WASHING A FLEECE

Many spinners dislike spinning greasy wool, but this does not apply to alpacas as their fibre contains no grease. But this grease does protect wool from weathering and contamination. And sheep don't roll in the dust and dirt as alpacas do. So although there is no grease to wash out, there is usually a lot of dust and grit. As mentioned previously, a good shake can remove much of this. If too much dust and grit are left in, this can damage your carding equipment, spread over you and your spinning wheel, and you can breathe in the dust from a really dusty fleece.

- The water need not be as hot as when washing wool as there is no grease to wash out. Two or three drops of eucalyptus oil added to the water aids dirt removal.
- As alpaca fibres usually contain more dirt and dust than wool, a long soak may be necessary to begin the washing process.
- Use the washing and drying method for wool, on page 97, but you may need to put the fibre in a large mesh bag as it is so soft and floaty. Change the water frequently.
- Make sure the washed fibre is thoroughly dry before storing.
- For suri fibre, the tight staple formation makes it harder for the water and detergent to penetrate. More detergent or longer immersion may be necessary.

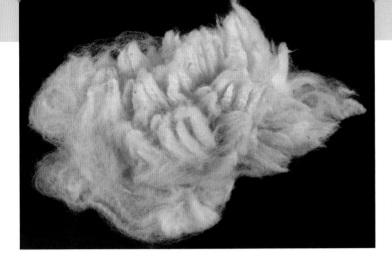

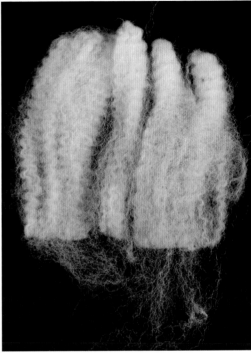

5.4 Huacaya fibre.

- As the two types of alpaca, huacaya and suri, are different fibre types, they look and behave very differently so we will look at the characteristics of each.

HUACAYA

Ninety per cent of alpacas are huacayas. Many breeders are selecting animals for breeding with a higher crimp count to give elasticity to the fibre as this is a desirable feature for weavers and knitters.

The micron range varies from as fine as 14 to more than 30, so choose your fibre to suit the end use. For finer, softer garments, move towards the lower range. Younger animals, such as cria, have softer, finer fibre as, with sheep, the fibre becomes coarser with age. Good quality alpaca will hold their micron count well into old age. Although alpaca fibre is usually more expensive than wool, it goes further, resulting in good value for money.

The length varies, depending on the frequency of shearing. Spinning is best done from fibre that is between 8–12cm (3–5in) long.

5.5 Heavily crimped huacaya fibre from Apollo, Highway Star Farm (see top photo 5.1 page 101).

CHARACTERISTICS OF HUACAYA ALPACA

- Soft and lightweight.
- Long fibre length.
- Silky, slippery, comfortable feel.
- Contains no grease.
- Strong.
- Lustrous, but not as lustrous as suri fibre.
- Feels warm.
- Dense.
- Excellent insulating qualities.
- Does not burn readily, burns slowly and leaves a crisp, shiny ash.
- Dyes easily and evenly.
- Crimped alpaca has good elasticity.

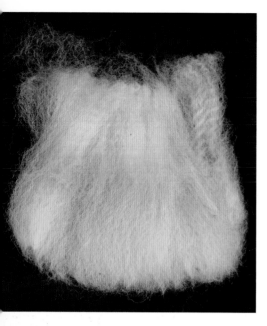

5.6 Flick-carded fibre.

SPINNING A YARN TO MATCH THE CHARACTERISTICS

Earlier I said that it is better to work with the fibre and not against it. The long fibres are easy to prepare and spin worsted and if spun fine the yarn will not be too heavy.

A cria fleece will give the finest and softest yarn. The yarn will be soft, silky, slippery, strong and lustrous, with no elasticity, all features of the fibre itself. A diluted, water-based oil product sprayed on a cria fleece while spinning can control and improve the end product and makes a finer, neater yarn.

COMMERCIALLY PREPARED FIBRE

For a true worsted yarn you will need tops or roving as the fibres will then be parallel, smooth and the same length. However, I have never found a commercially combed alpaca top preparation as all the commercially prepared fibre I have seen is carded, not combed.

PREPARING YOUR OWN FIBRE

For worsted yarn you will need to prepare the fibre with mini-combs (pages 54–55), flick carders or comb. Because alpaca is usually a long-stapled fibre, this is an easy method. Follow the instructions for flick-carding and combing on pages 56–57.

WORSTED SPINNING

Chapter 3 describes worsted spinning (see pages 24–26) and, with some adaptations, this method can be used for spinning alpaca. If you haven't spun alpaca before, it is a good idea to spin, ply and wash small sample skeins before you begin a project. Then you can make informed decisions about the type of yarn you want.

5.7 Worsted-spun alpaca yarn.

Huacaya fibre has a different scale structure to wool so it is smoother and more slippery. If you are more familiar with spinning wool, you will find that alpaca fibres tend to feel slippery and will draft more quickly than wool. Watch the amount of twist, both in the spinning and plying, because if you over-twist you will make the yarn stringy and uncomfortable to wear. As many breeders are now breeding for crimp and the fibre is becoming more elastic, these crimped fibres will hold their shape without adding extra twist.

As worsted yarn is spun from combed fibres which are parallel and have the shorter fibres removed in the preparation process, you can spin a lustrous, smooth yarn.

SURI

These animals are less common than huacaya and grow their fibre in long, lustrous, slippery staples which resemble dreadlocks. The micron range varies from 10–15. The fibre tends to look and behave more like a fine mohair.

5.8 Close-up of suri fibre, on the animal (Anne Rogers).

CHARACTERISTICS OF SURI ALPACA

- Very lustrous, more so than huacaya.
- Separate, thin curly locks that look like ringlets.
- No elasticity.
- Strong, long fibres.
- Smooth, slippery feel.
- No grease.
- Straighter fibre than huacaya.
- Cool to touch.
- Locks fall apart easily.
- Heavier than huacaya.

SPINNING A YARN TO MATCH THE CHARACTERISTICS

Again I would spin this fibre into a fine worsted yarn. Because the locks are long and separate, this is not an easy fibre to hand- or drum-card so flick-carding or combing for worsted yarn is the easiest. The yarn will be lustrous, smooth, slippery and strong with no elasticity. If the locks are too long, they can be cut to the required length.

Commercially prepared fibre

As these animals are not common, it will be hard to find some suri fibre that has been prepared for you. If you can acquire some, you will need tops or roving for a true worsted yarn as the fibres will then be parallel, smooth and the same length. Hold the fibre preparation up to the light to check.

5.9 Washed suri fibre.

5.10 (below) Washed, flick-carded and combed suri fibre.

Preparing your own fibre

For worsted yarn, you will need to prepare the fibre with flick carders or combs. Follow the instructions for flick-carding and combing on pages 54–57. Suri fibre, with its firm, ringlet formation, usually needs these ringlets opened before you can begin preparing it. Try pulling apart the tips, then flick-card or comb. For the yarn in photo 5.11, I did both. I flick-carded the locks, then combed them on my mini-combs, then pre-drafted from the combs through my diz.

Worsted spinning

If you have not spun suri alpaca before, it is a good idea to spin, ply and wash small sample skeins before you begin a project. As it is spun from combed fibres which are parallel and have the shorter fibres removed in the preparation process, you can spin a lustrous, smooth yarn. The lustre of suri is one of its most important characteristics, and spinning worsted will greatly enhance this feature.

Because the suri fibre in photo 5.9 was so long — 20cm (8in) — it was necessary to keep my hands well apart while drafting. A good guideline is that the longer the fibre, the further apart your hands should be.

Suri fibre is smoother and more slippery than huacaya so may need more twist. This also enhances the silk-like lustre of this fibre. Because there is no bulk, the yarn will not change with washing, so regulate the size so you do not end up with a heavy, dense yarn. If you want a thicker yarn, a three- or four-ply yarn will retain the lustre and light weight better than spinning a thicker two-ply yarn.

Because the fibre is inelastic, do not stretch it as you draft as this can cause the finished yarn to bubble slightly as it relaxes. To allow some air into the yarn as it is spun, fan the fibres out as you draft.

▮ PLYING

Make sure the plied alpaca yarn has sufficient twist. Remember that if you have spun the singles with more twist and then ply with too little twist, the yarn will be unbalanced and flat. The aim is a rounded yarn. For thicker yarn it is best to spin fine singles and then ply three or four together.

▮ WASHING THE YARN

Follow the instructions for washing yarn on pages 31–32. This will set the twist. Even if you have washed the fibre before preparation and spinning, the yarn needs that final wash. As alpaca has little or no bulk, the yarn size will not change with washing.

▮ USES
KNITTING

Good quality huacaya fibre is elastic and has crimp memory so will hold its shape well. Use a half-size smaller knitting needle for the cast on and ribbing. Alpaca yarn is suitable for people who can't wear wool next to their skin as it has no 'prickle' factor. This also makes it excellent for baby and children's garments.

Worsted-spun yarns are lustrous and show a very clear pattern definition and patterns, such as cables, lace patterns and Fair Isle, will show up well. Because the fibre is strong, this yarn makes excellent hard-wearing outdoor jerseys, gloves, mittens and hats, but the garments will still feel soft and light. Because of the lack of bulk compared to wool, the stitches should be close together for warmth, so use smaller needles than you would with wool yarn. This will also prevent the garment stretching with washing and wear.

5.11 Worsted-spun, three-ply suri yarn.

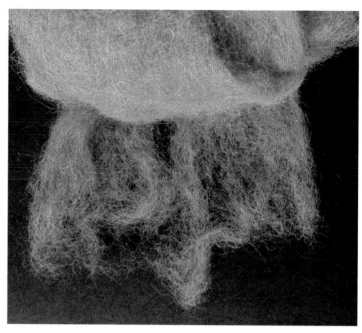

5.12 Commercially carded huacaya fibre.

5.13 (below) Hand-carded huacaya fibre.

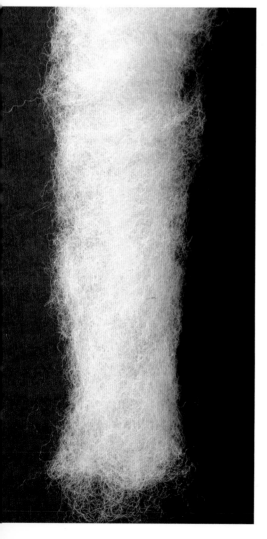

WEAVING

Alpaca fabric drapes well, so woven cloth has a good handle. The cloth will also be lustrous and soft and silky to touch. The fabric will also be lightweight so is ideal for blankets and throws. For a warp yarn, worsted-spun yarn is best as this will stand up to the abrasion in the heddles and reed.

▋ CHANGING THE CHARACTERISTICS

Earlier I said that it is easier to spin a yarn that enhances the original fibre properties, so I have devoted much of this chapter to spinning a worsted alpaca yarn with huacaya or suri fibre. However, there are ways to change the yarn structure so instead of spinning a smooth, lustrous worsted yarn, we can make the yarn softer and fluffier. It is the end project that will determine how you will need to spin the yarn.

For two different shawl types, a fine shawl knitted with an intricate pattern will need a fine worsted yarn for the pattern to show up clearly, however, a soft, fluffy shawl, in a thick yarn and knitted on large needles would be ideal for a woollen yarn.

Because suri alpacas are not as common and the difficulty of hand- and drum-carding this fibre with its separate ringlet staples, it is not an easy fibre for beginner spinners. When spinning woollen yarn, I suggest you choose huacaya fibre.

WOOLLEN SPINNING

Commercially prepared fibre

You will need a preparation method that has randomly arranged fibres of different lengths. Hold the fibres up to the light and see how they are arranged. See page 59 for more about this type of fibre preparation.

Preparing the fibre yourself

For woollen spinning, see the preparation methods for hand- or drum-carding on pages 60–62. There is more static in alpaca fibre than in wool so it is inclined to float off the carders. Using the brush on the drum carder (see page 62), is a help in anchoring the fibres onto the carding cloth. If the fibres are too long for hand- and drum-carding, cut them in half before carding.

Because there are such a wide variety of alpaca colours, blending on a drum or hand carders can be fun. Two similar colours will make an even colour blend, two more dissimilar colours, such as white and black, can produce a marled effect. If you card the fibres once, you get a striped batt. The more times you card the fibres, the more the colours blend.

Alpaca is often blended with other fibres such as silk and wool, as in Chapter 11.

Spinning

Woollen-spun yarn (see pages 64–67) from carded fibre makes a light, fluffier yarn containing the shorter fibres as these are not removed by this method of preparation. The dilemma is that these shorter fibres may shed from the finished article. The water-based oil spray mentioned earlier on page 104 will help control and retain the loft.

Uses

Woollen-spun yarns are not as hard-wearing as worsted-spun yarns and will fluff up with wear, and may felt with too much washing. Shawls and scarves are good projects for both knitting and weaving. The texture will obscure fancy patterns and, if knitted too loosely, garments will lose their shape, stretch and drop. So tension swatches are a good idea.

SEMI-WOOLLEN & SEMI-WORSTED YARNS

These spinning methods can also be used to spin alpaca fibre (see pages 58–68). Again spinning small sample skeins will help you choose the most suitable spinning method for your end project. The yarn in 5.16 (see page 112) was spun semi-worsted.

5.14 Woollen-spun huacaya yarn.

▦ PROJECTS

Woven beaded alpaca scarf
by Kaye Cooper

This scarf was spun and woven by Kaye Cooper, Australia, as part of a scarf-exchange project. These scarf exchanges have been happening for years. A guild hosts the event. A crafter sends 150gm (5.2oz) of clean prepared fibre to the host group. The fibre is then sent to other crafters, who may spin, weave, felt, knit, crochet or dye to create items, predominately scarves, which are returned to the host group. There is usually an exhibition, then the items are returned to the original fibre supplier. In 2010 there were over 150 entries from all over the world, and the theme was From the Forest to the Sea.

Fibre: Cria alpaca
Raw fibre weight: 120gm (4.2oz)
Preparation: The fibre was first washed in lukewarm water. When dry it was picked through to remove most of the debris. It was then carded into mini-batts, which were then pre-drafted (split and elongated) before spinning.
Spinning: The fibre was spun worsted with a relatively low spinning/plying twist to retain the handle.
Finished skein weight: 94gm (3.3oz)

5.15a Woven, beaded and dyed scarf.

5.15b Alpaca fibre, washed, pre-drafted and spun.

5.15c (below) Woven, beaded and dyed scarf detail.

Weaving

Structure: Undulating Twill, from Carol Strickler's book, *A Weaver's Book of 8 Shaft Patterns*, page 52, draft 221.

Equipment: 8-shaft loom, 40cm (16in) wide, one shuttle. 12-dent reed. Beads.

Warp and weft yarn: Handspun cria alpaca. 24 wraps per 2.5cm (1in).

Warp length: 1 scarf 140cm (55in) long, plus 10cm (4in) fringe each end.

Loom waste: 60cm (24in)

Total length of warp: 2m (80in); 168m (182yds)

Width in reed: 18cm (7in). Finished width 15cm (6in)

Sett: 12 ends per 2.5cm (1in)

Picks per 2.5cm (1in): 12

Weight of finished scarf: 91gm (3¼oz)

The beads were threaded onto invisible thread — about 250 at a time. The end of this thread was tied to an outside warp thread. After each 6th pick, the thread reel with all the beads was passed through the shed, leaving 4 or 5 for that pick, randomly spaced. The invisible thread was carried up the edge until the next 6th pick.

Dyeing: The finished scarf was dyed after weaving by painting it in a solid blue colour twice, then painted again to achieve some variation to represent the ocean. The dyes used were Landscape dyes from Kraftcolour.

Crocheted hoodie
Alpaca spun by Anne Field
Pattern adapted & crocheted by Doris O'Brien

5.16 Semi-worsted alpaca yarn.

Spinning: I spun this yarn semi-worsted from the alpaca fibre in photo 5.12 (page 108). The alpaca fibre was commercially carded and I then spun it worsted. Because the fibre was carded, it was randomly arranged and the subsequent yarn was lighter and contained more air than if it had been combed into a parallel form.

Plying: Normally most spinners spin the singles clockwise (Z twist) and ply anticlockwise (S twist). The action of crocheting untwists the ply slightly so it is best to spin the opposite way (singles S, ply Z). However, after 50 years of spinning one way, I find this very difficult. The minute my concentration lapses, I go back to my old habits. To counteract this, I plied with slightly more twist than normal, and assumed that the crocheting would undo some of this extra twist.

Yarn size: 14 wraps per 2.5cm (1in)
Amount of yarn: 500gm (18oz)
Weight of finished hoodie: 402gm (14oz)
Wraps per 2.5cm (1in): 14. The yarn was doubled for this project.
Tension: Diameter of centre circle: 11cm (4½in)
To fit: 81–91cm (32–36in) chest
Hook: 6.00mm (4)

Abbreviations
ch. = chain
d.c = double crochet
d.tr. = double treble
in = inch (English terms used)
sp. = space
s.s. = slip stitch
st/s = stitch/es
tr. = treble
tr.tr. = triple treble
Note: Use yarn double throughout. Work ch. between shells loosely.

Hoodie pattern
*** Using the yarn double make 5 ch., join in a ring with s.s. in first chain.
Round 1: 3 ch., work 15 tr. into ring, join with s.s. In top of 3 ch.: 16 sts.
Round 2: 4 ch. * 1 tr. in next stitch, 1 ch.: rep from * ending s.s. in 3rd of 4th ch.

Round 3: s.s. in first 1 ch. sp., 4 ch., 1 d.tr. in same 1 ch. sp., miss next 1 ch. sp., (2 d.tr., 2 ch., 2 d.tr.) in next 1 ch. sp., miss next 1 ch. sp., rep from * ending 2 d. tr. in first 1 ch. sp., 2 ch., s.s. in top of 4 ch.: 8 shells.

Round 4: s.s in 2 ch. sp. just made, 4 ch., 2 d.tr. in same 2 ch. sp., 1 ch., *(3 d.tr., 2 ch., 3 d.tr.) in next 2 ch. sp., 1 ch., rep from * ending 3 d.tr. in first 2 ch. sp., 2 ch., s.s. in top of 4 ch.

Round 5: s.s. in 2 ch. sp. just made, 4 ch., 2 d.tr. in same 2 ch. sp., (2 d.tr., 2 ch., 2 d.tr.) in next 1 ch. sp., *(3 d.tr., 2 ch. 3 d.tr.) in next 2 ch. sp., (2 d.tr., 2 ch., 2 d.tr.) in next 1 ch, sp., rep from * ending 3 d.tr. in first 2 ch. sp. 2 ch., s.s. in top of 4 ch.: 16 shells.

Round 6: s.s in 2 ch. sp. just made, 4 ch., 2 d.tr. in same 2 ch. sp., *(3 d.tr. 2 ch., 3 d.tr.) in next 2 ch. sp.; rep from * ending 3 d. tr. in first 2 ch. sp., 2 ch. s.s. in top of 4 ch.

Round 7: s.s in 2 ch. sp. just made, 4 ch., 2 d.tr. in same 2 ch. sp., 2 ch., *(3 d.tr., 2 ch., 3 d.tr.) in next 2 ch. sp., 2 ch., rep from * ending 3 d.tr. in first 2 ch. sp., 2 ch., s.s in top of 4 ch.

Round 8: s.s in 2 ch. sp. just made, 5 ch., 2 tr.tr. in same 2 ch. sp., 3 ch., miss next 2 ch. sp., *(3 tr.tr., 2 ch., 3 tr.tr.) in next 2 ch. sp., 3 ch., miss next 2 ch. sp., 3 ch., miss next 2 ch. sp.; rep from * ending in 3 tr.tr. in first 2 ch. sp., 2 ch., s.s in top of 5 ch.***

Work upper back as follows:

Row 1: Right side facing, 5 ch., 2 tr.tr in next st., 3 ch., *(3 tr.tr.,

2 ch., 3 tr.tr.) in next 2 ch. sp., 3 ch. * rep from * to * twice more, miss 5 tr.tr., 3 tr.tr. in next tr.tr. Turn: 3 shells and 2 half shells.

Row 2: 5 ch., 2 tr.tr. in first st., 3 ch., *(3tr.tr., 2 ch., 3 tr.tr.) in next 2 ch. sp., 3 ch., rep from * ending 3 tr.tr. in top of 5 ch.

Rep. last row 3 times more. Fasten off.

With right side facing, rejoin yarn in 7th tr.tr. from where work was turned and continue as follows:

Row 1: 5 ch., 2 tr.tr. in first st., 4 ch., *(3 tr.tr., 2 ch., 3 tr.tr.) in next 2 ch. sp., 4 ch. * rep from * to * 8 times more, miss 5 tr.tr., 3 tr.tr in next tr.tr. turn: 9 shells and 2 half shells.

Row 2: 5 ch., 3 tr.tr. in first st., 4 ch., *(4 tr.tr., 2 ch., 4 tr.tr.) in next 2 ch. sp., 4 ch.; rep from * ending in 4 tr.tr. in top of 5 ch.

Row 3: make 44 ch., turn, 3 tr.tr. in 6th ch. from hook, 5 ch., miss 12 ch., *(4 tr.tr., 2 ch., 4 tr.tr.) in next ch., 5 ch., miss 12 ch. * rep. from * to * once more, (4 tr.tr., 2 ch., 4 tr.tr.) in next st., 5 ch., **(4 tr.tr., 2 ch., 4 tr.tr.) in next 2 ch. sp., 5 ch., rep from ** ending (4 tr.tr., 2 ch., 4 tr.tr.) in top of 5 ch. Fasten off.

Rejoin yarn to top of 5 ch. just worked into and make 39 ch. Fasten off.

Rejoin yarn to top of last tr.tr., 5 ch., miss 12 ch., *(4 tr.tr., 2 ch., 4 tr.tr.) in next ch., 5 ch., miss 12 ch., * rep from * to * once more, 4 tr.tr. in last ch.: 15 shells and 2 half shells.

Row 4: 5 ch., 4 tr.tr. in first st., 5 ch., *(5 tr.tr., 2 ch., 5 tr.tr.) in

next 2 ch. sp., 5 ch.; rep from * ending 5 tr.tr. in top of 5 ch. Fasten off.
Shape neck as follows:
Row 5: With right side facing, miss 10 tr.tr. from where work was fastened off, rejoin yarn in next tr.tr., 5 ch.,
4 tr.tr. in same st., * 5 ch., (5 tr.tr., 2 ch., 5 tr.tr.) in next 2 ch. sp., * rep from * to * twice more, ** 7 ch., (5 tr.tr.,
2 ch., 5 tr.tr.) in next 2 ch. sp., ** rep from ** to ** 6 times more, then rep from * to * twice, 5 ch.,
miss 9 tr.tr., 5 tr.tr in next tr.tr. Fasten off.
Right side facing and neck edge, rejoin yarn then 5 ch., 4 tr.tr. in same st., 7 ch., then 5 tr.tr., 2 ch., 5 tr.tr. in
next 2 ch. space. 7 ch., then 5 tr.tr. in next 2 ch. sp. Fasten off . Repeat on other side.

Hood
Work as for pattern from *** to ***.
Next row: s.s into first tr.tr., 5 ch., 2 tr.tr. in this st., 3 ch., *(3 tr.tr., 2 ch., 3 tr.tr.) in next 2 ch. sp., 3 ch., *
rep from * to * 12 times more, miss 5 tr.tr., 3 tr.tr. In next tr.tr., turn: 13 shells and 2 half shells.
Next row: 5 ch., 2 tr.tr. in first st., 3 ch., *(3 tr.tr., 2 ch., 3 tr.tr.) in next 2 ch. sp., 3 ch.; rep from * ending in 3 tr.tr.
In top of 5 ch. Rep last row once more
Next row: 5 ch., 2 tr.tr. in first st., *(3 tr.tr., 2 ch., 3 tr.tr.) in next 2 ch. sp., rep from * ending last rep 3 tr.tr. in top
of 5 ch.
Next row: 1 ch., 1 d.c. in each of first 6 sts., * 1 d.c. in next 2 ch. sp., 1 d.c. in each of next 6 sts., rep from * to
end. Turn. 1 ch., 1 d.c. in each st. to end. Turn.
Next row: 1 ch., then 1 d.c. in next st. then picot, * 1 d.c. in next 2 sts. then picot, * rep to end of row.
Fasten off.

To make up
To prevent heavy pressing and use of a hot iron, finish as follows:
Block each piece by pinning out round edges and press using a warm iron and slightly damp cloth,
excluding d.c. border.
Using a flat seam, join front shoulders one and a half shells at back.

Finishing around armholes
With right side facing work 1 round d.c. around armholes, missing 1 st at front corner.
The 1 row picot as for hood.

Buttons
Three Dorset buttons (see below) were used in this garment, using the same yarn. However, other
buttons can be used. Sew buttons on front on half shell then on 1 shell, then on half shell. Other side
shells use as buttonholes.
Sew hood to neck edge with a flat seam.

SOURCES
Susan Wise, Highway Star Farm, Canterbury, New Zealand: highwaystar@paradise.net.nz
Susan also gave me valuable advice when I was writing this chapter.
Homestead Farm Alpaca Stud: www.homesteadfarm.co.nz
Dorset buttons: instructions for making these are readily available; just Google 'Dorset buttons' for options.

Silk

6

SILK HAS ALWAYS been thought of as a luxury fibre. The lustre and the smooth, slippery feel of the yarn makes silk garments something to treasure. Silk makes us look and feel good. In earlier centuries it was also a sign of wealth, and was worn by people who could afford the high cost. To describe something as silky is high praise.

Part of this magical appeal is because it was a mystery fibre to most of the world for 2000 years. China, the home of silk culture, protected its silk industry until about AD 300 when silk culture and processing gradually began to spread westwards.

Spinning this luxurious fibre is a real treat as it glides through your hands and looks and feels so smooth. If you have only spun wool or alpaca fibres, there are some major differences when spinning silk if you want to retain this special feel and handle. When I first tried spinning silk, the end result was a disappointment. The yarn was dull and lifeless, and I couldn't work out what I had done to change the beautiful fibre into such uninteresting yarn.

Thanks to silk experts such as Priscilla Lowry, I can now spin silk yarn with the same characteristics as the fibre.

Silk is a protein fibre. It is the filament made by silkworms when they spin their cocoons on the way to becoming silk moths. I wonder who first thought of unwinding (reeling), the silk from the cocoon to use as thread. The best quality comes from the unbroken cocoon so the chrysalis is killed inside the cocoons, which are then placed in very hot water to dissolve the sericin, a gum which makes the cocoons rigid.

6.1 (above) Silkworms, cocoon and moth and (left) dyed and undyed silk cocoons.

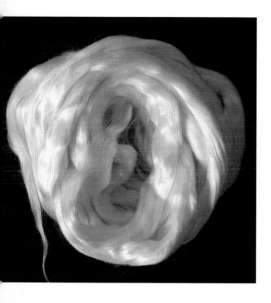

6.2 Bombyx silk fibre.

6.3 Tussah silk fibre.

It is the middle coat of the cocoon that produces the finest silk; the outer and inner layers are usually discarded. The filament is reeled off from 3–10 cocoons at once and one cocoon can contain about 1.6km (1 mile) of filament.

Silk comes in many forms. The two main types of silk used by spinners are bombyx or tussah silk top. Within these silk types, there will be a wide variety in the quality and this will affect how it is spun and what projects it is suitable for.

- Bombyx silk is cultivated and the pure white colour comes from its food — mulberry leaves. Because of the lack of pigmentation, bombyx silk dyes into clear, clean colours much prized in the industry. This silk is of the highest quality.
- Tussah silk means any silk that isn't bombyx. The cocoons are wild, not cultivated, are larger and the silk is not as fine or lustrous as bombyx. The colour ranges from pale to dark brown, and the yarn dyes without the clarity of the bombyx silk.

Silk is often blended with other fibres (see Chapter 11) to add lustre and strength.

CHARACTERISTICS OF SILK

- Lustrous.
- Strong.
- Doesn't pill.
- Long fibres.
- Doesn't felt.
- Soft, warm handle.
- Very little elasticity.
- Good insulator.
- No loft or bulk.
- Slippery.
- Ignites easily, self-extinguishing leaving a black, crisp ash.

SPINNING A YARN TO MATCH THE CHARACTERISTICS

Make sure the spinning wheel orifice is clean and free from grease and dirt as this can stain the yarn.

For a finished yarn that enhances these characteristics, spin combed silk top. This has been prepared so the fibres are long and parallel. Either bombyx or tussah is suitable, although bombyx will give a finer, more lustrous yarn. If this is the first time you have spun silk, you will find that tussah silk is slightly less slippery than bombyx silk and easier for a beginner.

Check the quality of the prepared fibre. A1 grade silk is the best. To test the quality, take a 20cm (8in) length between your two hands and gradually pull it apart. As it becomes thinner you can see the fibre length, the lustre and whether the fibres are the same length, lying parallel and whether there are any short fibres or noils. For spinning, a fibre length of between 8-15cm (3-6in) is best.

■ SPINNING

Break the tops into about 30cm (12in) lengths and then split this shorter length into about 3–4 thinner portions lengthways. To break off a length from the tops, hold your hands about 30–40cm (12–15in) apart and give a sharp tug. If your hands are too close together, it is impossible to break. Silk tops are very compact and because they are so strong and the fibres are long, the fibre very quickly becomes a solid, immoveable mass and drafting becomes impossible.

To make a light, smooth and lustrous yarn, spin worsted (see page 57). The evident twist in worsted yarn makes a very lustrous yarn. And never wear velvet or corduroy clothing while spinning. Silk seems to have a strong attachment to these fabrics and I end up with more on me than in the yarn. With worsted spinning the twist doesn't get past the front hand. If this happens when spinning the very strong fibres of silk, drafting will be impossible. Because silk feels so slippery and has no scales, you feel it should be easy to draft and just slide past your fingers. But the second the fibres are twisted it becomes a strong, compacted yarn which won't draft at all.

Because silk fibre has no bounce or loft, worsted silk yarn can feel solid and flat, so try to get some air into the fibre as it is drafted. If you are used to spinning wool, you will notice a big difference. Wool spun into a fine worsted yarn with lots of twist will still feel soft.

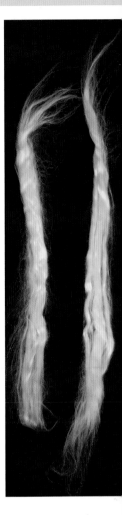

6.4 (above) Silk top (pulled apart).

6.5 (above right) Pre-drafted tops ready for spinning.

6.6 (left) Spinning silk yarn.

6.7 Silk skeins, bombyx (right) and tussah (left).

Silk, if spun exactly the same, will feel stringy and harsh, with little lustre and garments made from it will quickly lose their shape.

Spin as for worsted yarn but hold the fibres in the back hand so they open out into a fan shape. Your hands should be further apart than when spinning worsted wool. This will let some air into the fibres as they are drafted. Spin with slightly less twist than for a wool worsted yarn to make a soft, light yarn. Your back hand opens and fans the fibre out. The thumb of my back hand seems to do most of this opening out.

Because the fibre is so slippery, make the joins very firm. I join the old and the new fibres together for about 10–13cm (4–5in).

PLYING

To make a rounded, lightweight yarn, ply with *more* twist than you would when plying a wool yarn. The singles should be slightly under-twisted; the plied yarn should be slightly over-twisted. Silk is so strong that a singles can be used on its own but the twist and size need to be consistent, which may be difficult for a beginner spinner.

WASHING

Wash the skeins in hand-hot, soapy water. Use a good quality hand or dishwashing liquid, not a soap powder. Don't soak the skeins. Squeeze the water out, then rinse two or three times in warm water.

You can add a drop of vinegar or baby oil to the water at this stage. Don't wring the skein but wrap it in a towel and squeeze the excess water out. Wet silk doesn't look appealing but don't worry what it looks like at this stage. Shake the skein well and hang out of direct sunlight to dry. Shake or snap the skein several times while it is drying. When the skein is almost dry, you can beat the skein against a smooth surface like a chair back (a good exercise if you are in a bad mood), or put the skein in a bag in a tumble drier for a few minutes on a medium heat. You will be surprised how this treatment transforms your dull, flat skeins into light, lustrous yarn.

▓ USES

KNITTING

Silk yarn has little elasticity and will not stretch, but it will drop so knit on needles two times finer than you would for an equivalent wool yarn. Tension squares are important. Measure these squares before and after washing and note the changes. And remember that wet silk is unappealing. A good shaking now and then while drying your tension swatch helps. Then make your decision about which tension and needle size is best.

Ribbing needs to be even firmer and on smaller needles than is usual, or other types of edging such as a hemmed edge can be used. When making a hemmed edge, again use needles two times smaller than the body of the garment. Using knitting elastic knitted in with the silk yarn will add elasticity to bands. Lace patterns will stretch and drop more than other patterns.

Excellent advice for knitting with silk yarn can be found in Priscilla Lowry's book *The Secrets of Silk: From Textiles to Fashion*, Chapter Ten.

WEAVING

Silk fabric drapes well with a soft, smooth handle. Sett the yarn closer together in the warp and weft than you would for wool yarns. Patterns will show up clearly. One of my most successful scarves was woven with a lustrous warp of bombyx silk, and a dull weft of silk noil. The colour distinction was subtle with the pattern showing as the cloth moved. Handspun silk also makes an excellent embroidery yarn.

▓ CHANGING THE CHARACTERISTICS

Bombyx and tussah silk spin into smooth, lustrous yarns with the same characteristics of the original fibre. However, by spinning other silk preparations, you can make lovely textured yarn.

Problem solving

- **The fibres will not draft.**
  Solution: The twist may have got past your front hand and into the drafting zone. Stop and unwind the fibre before beginning to spin again. It is almost impossible to break silk once it has been twisted so unwinding is the best option. You can also feed in the yarn faster and treadle slower.

- **The yarn feels stringy and hard.**
  Solution: You may be putting too much twist into the yarn. Spin with less twist and make sure the fibres are fanned out in your relaxed back hand.

- **The fibres in your back hand are tangled and not flowing smoothly.**
  Solution: You may be holding too much fibre in your back hand. Reduce the amount and don't hold the fibre so tightly that your hands get sticky.

- **The spun yarn breaks frequently.**
  Solution: Check that there is enough twist in the yarn. When joining the yarn, overlap the fibres by at least 10–13cm (4–5in).

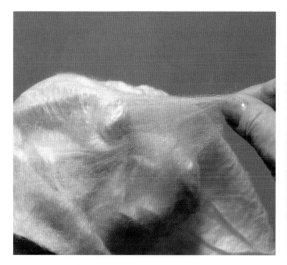

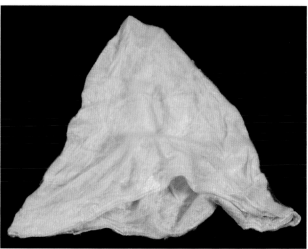

6.8 Silk cap.

MAWATA SILK CAPS & HANDKERCHIEFS

Caps are round, handkerchiefs are square. This fibre comes from broken cocoons that have been soaked in very hot water to remove the sericin. The cocoons are then opened, the pupa is removed, and the cocoons are stretched in layers on a frame to dry.

By using silk caps or handkerchiefs we can change the characteristics of silk to make a more textured, less lustrous yarn that is still strong. The fibres will contain some waste. This silk preparation is usually dyed and the colours are brilliant. Both caps and handkerchiefs are treated the same.

Preparation

It is amazing how much fibre comes out of one cap or handkerchief. There are usually between 8–15 layers but a full cap can have up to 30 layers. To pull them apart, put one hand into the cap and hold all the fibres except the outside layer with the fingers and thumb of that hand. With the other hand, pinch the outside layer. Snap your hands apart and the top layer peels off. This layer can then be spun without any further preparation. The fibres will catch on any rough surface, so if I have been gardening without gloves, I may need to put hand cream (rubbed well in) or talcum powder on my hands before spinning.

Spinning

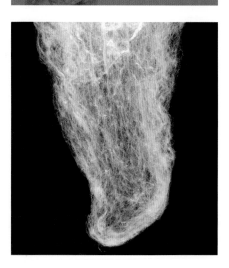

6.9 a, b & c Separating a cap or handkerchief.

If spun worsted (see page 57), the yarn is smoother and more solid. Because of the strength of the fibres, I find it difficult to spin caps woollen. Keep your hands well apart to allow the fibres to slip past each other as you draft. Leave the noils in as this adds to the texture.

Uses
Knitting

This yarn is ideal for scarves and shawls where the texture will show to the best advantage.

Weaving

This is best used for a weft yarn, and the surface weave pattern on page 35 would show this to great advantage. A worsted-spun silk warp and this yarn as a weft make an excellent combination.

SILK NOIL
Silk noil is short, broken fibres left after the best silk has been processed. It doesn't have the lustre and strength of bombyx and tussah silk. It can even contain little black specks, which are bits of the last skin shed by the silk worm. It is greyish in colour, dull and short but dyes well and doesn't slip easily. If it is not already carded, you can card it yourself.

The lumps and bumps are part of this yarn and even if spun worsted (see page 57), you get a textured yarn. Textured is really a polite way of saying your yarn is rough and lumpy!

Woollen-spun (see page 64) silk noil makes a really textured yarn, but the fibre will need to be open and able to flow freely. If it doesn't flow freely, hand card the fibre, even although it may have been carded previously. This will open up the fibres. One single of silk noil and one single of bombyx or tussah silk plied together makes an interesting novelty yarn.

6.10 Yarn spun from silk caps.

Uses
Knitting

This yarn will not be as strong or hard-wearing as other silk yarns, so is best used for scarves and shawls.

Weaving

Don't use this yarn as a warp because it won't be strong or smooth enough. It makes an interesting textured weft yarn.

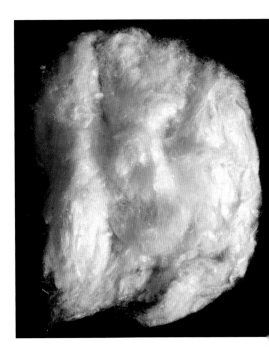

6.11 Silk noil.

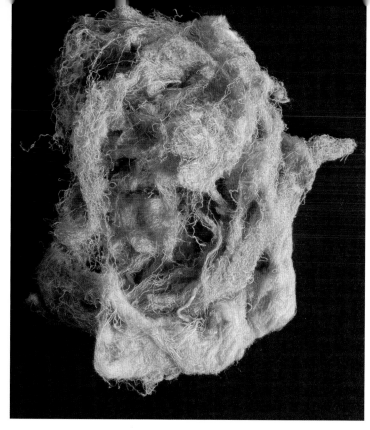

6.12 Dyed throwsters silk.

6.13 (below) Yarn spun from throwsters silk.

THROWSTERS SILK

This is waste silk and is a tangled mass of short, crimpy fibres. Cut the fibres before spinning into 5–8cm (2–3in) lengths, clipping any knots to open them up as well, and put them into a container on your lap. Make the most of this bouncy, springy fibre by spinning it into a bouncy, springy yarn. Don't try to smooth or tidy the fibres, just spin as quickly as possible with lots of twist, using a worsted or woollen spinning method. The finished yarn should resemble bouclé yarn. In photo 6.13 I plied it with a matching polyester sewing thread. The spool of sewing thread was placed on a lazy kate and I plied the two threads together with a lot of twist.

Throwsters silk can also be blended on hand or drum carders with other fibres such as alpaca or wool. Again it will need cutting up first.

Uses

It makes an interesting novelty yarn when used as a feature in weaving or knitting. Knitting or weaving a couple of rows of this yarn gives an interesting texture to a border when changing a colour or pattern.

▓ PROJECTS

Knitted silk scarf
Spun by Anne Field
Knitted by Mary Catharine Jackson

The handspun tussah silk used in this scarf is the same as the tussah silk yarn in photo 6.7 (page 120).

Wraps per 2.5cm (1in): 16
Weight of finished scarf:
140gm (5oz)
Needle size: 4mm (US 5, UK 8).
Pattern stitch: Fluted Rib, from *A Second Treasury of Knitting Patterns* by Barbara Walker, Schoolhouse Press, 1998, page 5.

Cast on 47 sts — long tail cast on was used.
Maintain 3 sts on each edge in a garter stitch border. Slip the last stitch of every row as if to purl.
Knit into the back of the first stitch on each row.
Knit 3 ridges (6 rows) garter stitch for the border.
Multiple of 8 sts plus 1.
Rows 1, 2, and 3: P1, *K7, P1; repeat from *.
Row 4: K2, *P5, K3; rep from *, end P5, K2.
Row 5: P3, *K3, P5; rep from *, end K3, P3.
Rows 6, 7, and 8: K4, *P1, K7; rep from *, end P1, K4.
Row 9: Repeat Row 5.
Row 10: Repeat Row 4.
Repeat Rows 1–10.
Knit 3 ridges (6 rows garter stitch for border. Cast off. K2tog, place stitch back on left needle. Repeat from *.

When this scarf was washed, the ridged texture was flattened. If you want the ridges to be pronounced, don't wash.

6.14 Knitted silk scarf (above) and detail (left).

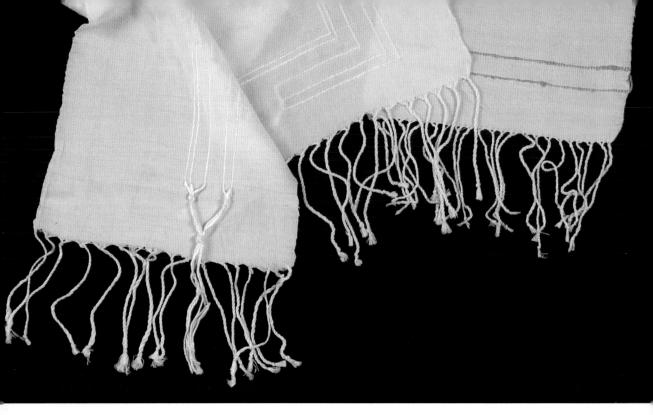

Woven silk scarves
by Anne Field

I wanted the handspun silk to add texture to these scarves. Therefore the warp and weft yarns were very fine silk to emphasise the different textures. The designs I chose showed the four types of handspun silk to advantage. The warp was the same for all four scarves. These scarves could also be woven on a rigid heddle loom.

Equipment: 4-shaft loom, 40cm (16in) wide, one shuttle. 12-dent reed.

Warp and weft yarn: 60/2 silk

Warp length: As I wove four scarves, each 1.8m (6ft) long, with a 15cm (6in) fringe at each end, on one warp, the warp length was:

Scarf warp (including fringes): 8m (8½yds)

Loom waste: 60cm (24in)

Total length of warp: 8.6m (9½yds)

Width in reed: 20cm (8in)

Sett: 48 ends per 2.5cm (1in)

Picks per 2.5cm (1in): 60

Weight of finished scarf: 28gm (1oz)

Structure: Plain weave

Weaving: After threading the loom and before beginning weaving scarf one and two, I added a stronger silk thread at each selvedge and weighed these two ends separately at the back of the loom. For scarves three and four, I added a weighted lurex end at each selvedge instead of the thicker silk.

SCARF 1: HANDSPUN BOMBYX SILK
Photo 6.7, page 120 as the pattern yarn

I wove 5cm (2in) of plain weave, then measured out 5 lengths of the handspun bombyx silk, each 2.5m (8ft) long. I placed these extra warp ends through the heddles and reed alongside the fine silk warp ends and attached them to the weaving with a figure of eight around a pin. At the back of the loom, I weighed these 5 ends so they were the same weight as the rest of the warp. The back of the loom did look rather untidy at this stage, with all my weighted ends dangling down. Starting the handspun silk warps ends 5cm (2in) in from the scarf end emphasised these thicker ends.

I wove for 160cm (5½ft), then cut each of the 5 handspun ends in turn and wove them in as weft. Again this made these ends into a strong design element, and gave the scarf a different look at each end. The fringe was twisted.

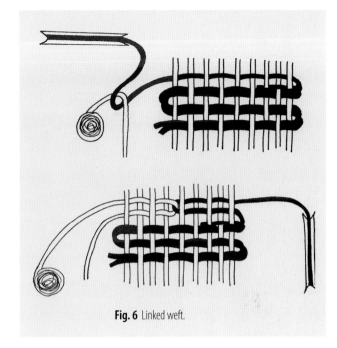

Fig. 6 Linked weft.

SCARF 2: YARN SPUN FROM SILK CAPS
Photo 6.10, page 123 as the pattern yarn

The pattern yarn used in this scarf was the textured yarn spun from silk caps. I threaded this as a warp end in the centre of the warp alongside an existing thread through the same heddle and reed dent and weighed it at the back of the loom.

When I wanted to turn this warp end into a weft yarn, I put the shuttle through the warp, around the pattern end, then returned the shuttle to the side it came from, dragging this warp with it. Without changing sheds, I threw the shuttle through to the other side. I repeated this, alternating right and left sides. This technique is called linked weft (see Fig. 6), or meet and separate. The beginning and end of this scarf was hemstitched.

SCARF 3: THROWSTERS WASTE
Photo 6.13, page 124 as the pattern yarn

For the pattern stripes at the beginning and end of this scarf, I used the dyed throwsters waste as the weft as it was too thick to fit through the heddles or reed dents.

SCARF 4: UNSPUN SILK AS THE PATTERN YARN

Every now and then I put a small folded piece of dyed silk sliver through the shed with a normal silk weft in the 60/2 silk. I dyed the sliver with Earth Palette dyes.

SOURCES
Fibre source: Karen Selk, www.treewaysilks.com
Earth Palette Dyes: cdouglass@paradise.net.nz

6.15b Scarves 2 & 4.

Mohair

7.1 Angora goat.

7.2 (below) Kid mohair, washed.

MOHAIR IS THE fibre that comes from angora goats. These goats originated in Ankara, Turkey, hence the name. Because of the confusion with the angora rabbit, the goats' name has recently been officially changed to mohair. Now many countries in the world have large numbers, with South Africa producing 60% of the world's mohair. As the popularity of the fibre grew, pure-bred angora goats were crossed with common goats.

There are many varieties of mohair. The fibre can be used for carpets, upholstery, clothing and knitting yarns. In the 1960s, mills developed a looped mohair yarn which can be brushed to produce a soft fluffy yarn and this new yarn widened the use of mohair even further.

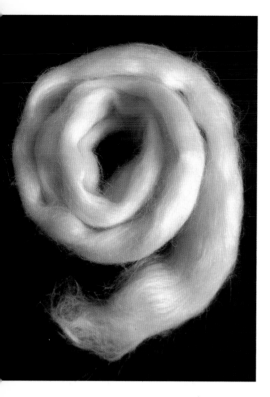

7.3 Commercially prepared mohair tops.

Mohair is a protein fibre, as is wool, and is similar to wool in structure, but without the crimp and with little scale structure. It resembles the long-wool breeds of sheep, such as the Leicesters and Wensleydale, as the locks have a similar wavy appearance. The average fibre diameter ranges from 24–48 micron, but kid mohair can be as fine as 18 micron. There is about 5% grease content.

Traditionally the fibre is white but naturally coloured goats are now being bred, primarily for the craft market. Kid mohair, the finest, comes from the baby goat but is also a term used for indicating the degree of fineness, so an older goat can produce kid mohair. The formation of locks in the form of ringlets is a good indication that the fibre is fine.

Goats are very hardy animals and will eat a variety of vegetation. Their diet has also been known to include clothes off a washing line so they are not fussy eaters.

SHEARING

One goat can produce 5–8kg (11–17lb) of mohair a year. The fleece grows about 30cm (12in) a year and is generally shorn twice a year as the resulting shorter fibres are easier to spin. As the goats are so active and can leap quite a distance, the shearing shed barriers are higher than when shearing sheep. I can remember watching the shearing of a flock of 2000 goats in the Nelson area in New Zealand, and the noise the goats made was so unlike sheep. It sounded more like babies crying.

SKIRTING

This is similar to skirting wool (see page 95). Again be sure to remove all the dirty, stained portions of the fleece. Also remove any parts that are contaminated with vegetable matter or have a very different appearance to the rest of the fleece.

CHARACTERISTICS OF MOHAIR FIBRE

- High lustre.
- Elastic, can stretch up to 30% but will spring back.
- Long fibres.
- Low felting and shrinking properties.
- Drapes well.
- Dyes well.
- Strong and durable.
- Wrinkle resistant.
- Good insulating qualities.
- Absorbs and releases moisture easily.
- Burns only in the flame, not out of it.

WASHING A FLEECE

This is the same method used for washing fleece wool (see page 97). However, the staples are more separate and won't cling together in the way staples from sheep fleeces do. Using a mesh basket will help to keep the fleece together.

SPINNING A YARN TO MATCH THE CHARACTERISTICS

To preserve the lustre, this fibre is best spun worsted. Usually the staples are long, which also makes it ideal for this spinning method. However, other spinning methods will be discussed later in this chapter.

PREPARATION
COMMERCIALLY PREPARED FIBRE

Mohair is available in sliver form. Hold the sliver up to the light and gently pull it apart lengthways to see how the fibres are arranged. If they are parallel and of the same length, the fibre preparation is suitable for worsted spinning, which will highlight the lustre.

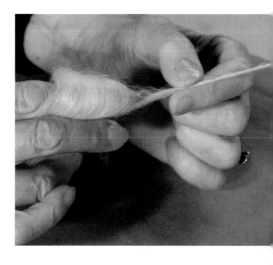

7.4 Spinning from the fold.

7.5 Yarn spun from commercially prepared tops.

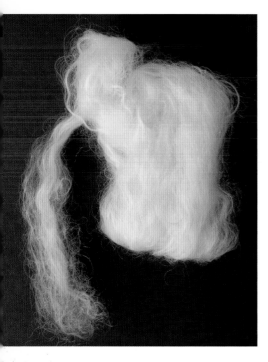

7.6 Pre-drafted flick-carded and combed fibre ready to spin.

7.7 Worsted spun and dyed yarn.

Spinning

I spun these tops worsted, but by breaking off about 12–15cm (5–6in) of the tops, folding this section over my forefinger and spinning it from the fold (see photo 7.4, page 131), I gave the yarn more bulk and springiness. The yarn was still lustrous and hard-wearing, but somewhat heavy because of the thicker yarn diameter. A thinner yarn would have less weight. If I had spun three thinner singles and then plied them together, I would have made a lighter yarn.

PREPARING THE FIBRE YOURSELF

As mohair, particularly kid mohair, may have a separate lock formation, prepare these locks in two stages. For this sample, I first lightly flick-carded the locks to open up the tips, then used the mini-combs (see page 54) and a diz. This gave a very smooth, parallel, pre-drafted fibre which was a joy to spin. For this type of preparation, the locks need to be longer than 8cm (3in). Any shorter and flick-carding is hazardous as you flick-card your hand as well.

Spinning

Spin worsted (see page 57). However, if you spin this fibre too fine with a lot of twist, you will end up with strong string. I know, I have done this. Of course it is very lustrous and strong and would make a good carpet warp, but it will be unwearable. As with silk it is best to spin the single with slightly less twist, but ply with slightly more.

Uses
Knitting

This yarn will allow lace and other fancy patterns to show up well. It is very hard-wearing and strong, so socks would be ideal. (see the sock project at the end of this chapter). Lacy shawls are another good choice. Knit on smaller needles than you would use with the fluffier, soft mohair yarns.

Weaving

Again lace patterns will show up well, It would make an excellent upholstery fabric and would also be suitable for outer wear, such as skirts, jackets and coats. Sett the yarns close together.

▨ CHANGING THE CHARACTERISTICS

To make a softer yarn, you will lose some of the lustre but will make up for this by spinning a yarn with a wide range of uses. This fibre can be spun semi-worsted, semi-woollen or woollen.

COMMERCIALLY PREPARED FIBRE

Check how the fibre has been prepared. Again, try pulling the fibre preparation slowly apart to see how the fibres are arranged and how long they are. If the fibres are randomly arranged with both short and long fibres, as in photo 7.8, you can spin semi-worsted or woollen.

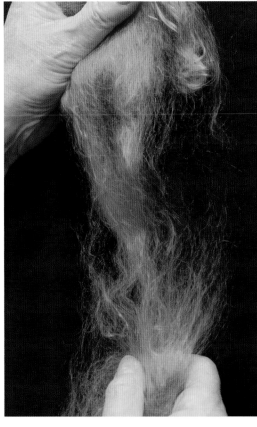

7.8 (above) Carded fibre.

7.9 Woollen spun yarn from carded mohair.

133

7.10 Separating the locks.

7.11 Carded rolags.

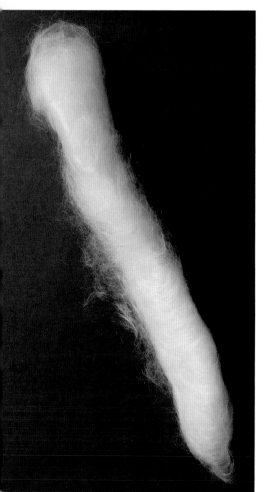

Spinning

To enhance the curly nature of this fibre, it can be spun woollen. Spin quickly and resist the temptation to remove the noils and shorter, curly fibres and you will make a yarn that is soft and lofty. The yarn spun in photo 7.9 (page 133), was spun from fibre pulled lengthwise off the prepared batt as I wanted the yarn for a woven scarf (see photo page 137). This made the yarn smoother, more resistant to abrasion and more suitable for weaving than if I had made rolags from the batt. Spinning from the rolags would have made a more open and fluffier yarn for knitting.

There are so many choices with the preparation and spinning that it helps in the decision-making to know the end use before you start.

PREPARING THE FIBRE YOURSELF

Washing the fibre (see photo 7.2, page 129) before starting the preparation will make this task easier. For a soft yarn, prepare the fibre with hand or drum carders (see pages 60–62). If the locks are in separate ringlets, you may need to separate the locks first and even flick-card before drum- or hand-carding if the ringlets persist in clinging together. If the fibres are too long to hand- or drum-card — that is, they are long enough to hang over the width of the hand carder — cut them in half first.

Spinning

Woollen spinning (see page 64), from hand-carded or drum-carded rolags, makes a lovely soft, curly yarn. To keep a light, open yarn, spin

7.12 Woollen yarn.

and ply with less twist. Mohair is a strong fibre and can be spun with less twist than a similar wool.

The fibre can also be from fibres prepared on hand or drum carders but spun worsted (see page 58). This will make a fairly smooth, light semi-worsted yarn but with some air.

For a novelty yarn, the ringlets are not separated completely in the preparation, leaving a slightly textured preparation with some parts light and fluffy and some wavy, partially opened sections. This yarn, if it is spun with little twist, can resemble looped mohair. The finished knitting or weaving can be brushed to raise the pile. (See Chapter 12, pages 189–195 for more novelty yarns.)

Uses
Knitting

For these lighter, fluffier mohair yarns, knit with larger needles than with the worsted mohair yarns. Shawls and scarves, jerseys, hats and mittens are suitable end uses. Blankets and throws also make good uses of this lightweight yarn.

Weaving

This yarn makes good blankets and throws, scarves and shawls. Sett the warp yarn further apart than usual as otherwise the warp ends will stick together. A sizing agent that can be washed out after weaving can help to keep the warp yarns separate while weaving.

■ PROJECTS

Knitted socks
by Sandra Dain

I worsted-spun this yarn (see photo 7.7, page 132) for the socks from the fibre in photo 7.6 (page 132). Sandra Dain dyed it using Terri dyes. Sandra is such an experienced sock knitter that she drew around my bare foot, then knitted to fit me. Weight of finished socks: 90gm (3oz).

Basic sock pattern

Adapted from *Blendy Knits Socks* by Belinda Too, with her kind permission. Use 4 needles.

Abbreviations

K = knit
P = purl
sl = slip
sts = stitches
tog = together

Cuff

Cast on 60 sts with 2.75mm (US 1–2, UK 11–12) needles, divide between 3 needles and knit 20 rows in K1 P1 rib.

Leg

Change to stocking stitch and knit 60 rows — about 20cm (8in) from the rib.

Heel

Knit 30 sts and leave the other 30 for the front of the sock.
Row 1: sl.1, purl to end.
Row 2: sl.1, knit to end.
Repeat the above 2 rows 13 times, then Row 1 once (29 rows in all).

Turning the heel

Row 1: sl.1, K17, ssk, K1 (ssk = slip 2 sts from left to right needle, put them back on the left needle the other way and knit them together), turn.
Row 2: sl.1, P4, P2tog, P1, turn.
Row 3: K5, ssk, K1.
Repeat rows 2 and 3 (knitting or purling one more stitch each time) until 18 sts are left.
While doing the following, you need to get back onto 3 needles, needle 2 having the front 30 sts.
Pick up 16 sts from the heel flap (avoid holes by picking up one near the front sts). Knit the 30 front sts, then pick up 16 sts from the heel flap.
The front sts should be on needle 2 and the side sts on 1 and 3.

Gusset

Knit to within 3 sts of the end of the first needle, K2tog, K1.
Knit across the front sts.
K1, ssk, knit to the end.
Continue as above until you are back to 60 sts.
Knit straight until the desired foot length is reached minus about 5cm (2in). At this stage it is possible to try on the sock carefully.

Toe

Row 1: Knit to within 3 sts of the end, K2tog, K1 (needle 1). Needle 2: K1, ssk, knit to within 3 sts of the end, K2tog, K1. Needle 3: ssk, knit to the end.
Row 2: Knit.
Repeat the above 2 rows until 24 sts remain.
With 12 sts on 2 needles, graft the sts together.

Woven mohair scarf
by Anne Field

The yarn used in this scarf is described on page 134 and in photo 7.9 (page 133). Again a rigid heddle loom with large holes and slots can be used. It is a quick project.

Structure: Plain weave
Equipment: 4 shaft loom, minimum width 30cm (12in) wide, one shuttle. 5 dent reed
Warp and weft yarn: 200gm (7oz) handspun mohair. 10 wraps per 2.5cm (1in)
Warp length: 2.5m (8ft); 50 ends
Width in reed: 25cm (10in)
Sett: 5 ends per 2.5cm (1in). 1 per dent in 5 dent reed
Picks per 2.5cm (1in): 5
Weight of finished scarf: 160gm (6oz)
Weaving: Weave in plain weave for the warp length. I knotted both ends of the scarf after removing it from the loom. I hand-washed the fabric in warm soapy water, rinsed it, and dried it lying flat. Don't press as this will flatten the texture.

Mohair squares
Woven on a 20cm (8in) frame loom by Margaret Dirago

These small looms are fun to use as they are so portable. Several years ago I wove a mohair throw on a similar square frame and crocheted it together. I gave it to my daughter, who stored it in a cupboard, away from her cat. It seems such a coincidence that Margaret and I used the same type of yarn, and the same sized squares. So the throw emerged from the cupboard to be photographed for this book to show you what the finished project looks like.

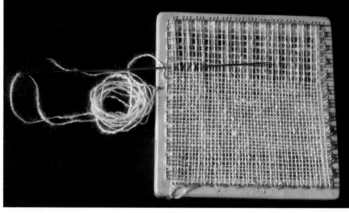

7.13 (above) Detail of mohair throw.

7.14 (top right) Weaving on the frame.

7.15a & b Finished squares (right), and finished mohair throw (opposite page).

Angora rabbit

8.1 Angora rabbit.

8.2 (below) Angora fibre.

THE ANGORA RABBIT originated in Ankara, Turkey, along with the angora goat. There is even an angora cat! This rabbit is bred mainly for its fibre, which is long and silky. It is a hair fibre, not wool, with long, smooth scales and air pockets which make it a very light fibre and provide excellent insulation. Top quality fibre can be 6.2–7.5cm (2½–3in) long and 13 micron in size. Because of the soft, silky feel of this fibre it is often described as fur. It is the longer guard hairs protruding from the softer, finer undercoat that give the rabbit its halo appearance. Along with the soft undercoat and the longer guard hairs there are also erector hairs, which help keep the animal warm. The animals resemble a fluffy ball when they have been groomed, a necessity as the fibre can easily become matted and felted. To groom the animals they can be brushed or their coats opened by blowing. It is one of the lightest, warmest fibres available to hand spinners.

The fibre can be clipped or plucked. Spinners prefer the plucked fibre as it seems to shed less than clipped fibre. It can be plucked in the normal shedding cycle of the rabbit, which happens twice a year for three weeks at a time. Clipping should take place every 12–13 weeks. Some spinners have an allergic reaction to the fibre; if so, try washing the fibre before spinning as it usually is a reaction to rabbit saliva, rather than the fibre itself.

8.3 Angora and merino yarn spun by Elaine Watkins.

There is a wide range of colours, although the most common one is white.

There are three main types of rabbits that produce fibre suitable for hand spinners. However, much cross breeding has taken place. For example, the Satin angora is a cross between a Satin and French angora.

- English angora: These are the smallest in size and have the softest coats, with little guard hair. English angora rabbits have growths of hair on the ears and the entire face except above the nose and on their legs. Because their hair coat is very thick, they need grooming twice a week.

- French angora: These rabbits are larger and have more guard hair with a soft undercoat. They have no hair on their faces or legs, and therefore require less grooming than the English angora. The guard hairs should be removed before spinning.

- German angora: These are the largest rabbits, usually weighing between 2–5.5kg (4.4–12lb) with a coarser fibre than the other two types. Again, the guard hairs should be removed before spinning. They are always white, whereas the English and French rabbits come in a variety of colours.

CHARACTERISTICS OF ANGORA RABBIT FIBRE

- Short fibre length, compared to other fibres.
- Lightweight.
- Very soft and silky.
- Felts very well.
- Dyes well.
- No oil or grease.
- Excellent insulating qualities.
- Fine fibre.
- No elasticity.

8.4 Angora yarn spun by Elaine Watkins.

SPINNING A YARN TO MATCH THE CHARACTERISTICS

For the beginner spinner, angora blended with other fibres is a good way to start, as in this sample skein spun with 40% German angora and 60% merino (see photo 8.3). If you have access to fibre that is about 7–8cm (3in) long, try spinning it on its own. After spinning and with washing and handling, the angora fibres work their way to the surface and create a halo effect around the spun yarn.

PREPARATION

The best way to prepare this fibre is to do nothing. Because it is such a fine, light fibre, it has a tendency to fly off the hand or drum carders (unless it is blended with wool). So to spin this fibre on its own, just choose clean fibre that is as long as possible.

SPINNING

Because of the relative shortness of this fibre, and to maintain the soft, fluffy appearance, try spinning a woollen-spun yarn, as on page 64. The fibres will feel slippery, and the secret is to put enough twist in to hold them together but not enough to make the yarn lose its soft, fluffy appearance.

8.5 Carded English angora dyed with acid dye and spun skein by Elaine Watkins.

If the fibres are long enough and you find woollen-spun yarn isn't firm enough, try worsted spinning (see page 57).

Ply together as normal. It is a good idea to sample with small skeins first as after plying and washing it is easy to see whether the yarn has enough strength to hold together. Also the fuzziness of the yarn doesn't show up until it is washed.

SPINNING AROUND A CORE

This is a good way to make a stronger yarn, but still with a soft, fluffy appearance. Take a ball of fine, soft wool yarn: a merino yarn is the best choice. This could also be a very fine hand-spun yarn, but for the beginner spinner, a commercially spun yarn is quicker.

Check which way it is plied. The merino yarn I used as the core yarn in photos 8.6 and 8.7 was a three-ply yarn, TEX110/3 (4800yd/lb), and it was plied Z. See page 31 for S and Z twists. I spun the angora onto the core S with the wheel going anticlockwise. This meant I undid some of the twist in the merino yarn as I spun. This made it easier for the angora to catch onto the core yarn. If I had spun Z, I would have added twist to the core yarn making it firmer and harder for the angora to catch on.

Put the ball of wool in a bowl or container near the foot of the spinning wheel. Join this onto the bobbin leader, then hold this yarn in one hand and feed it onto the bobbin, at the same time adding the angora fibre with the other hand. Keep the core yarn taut, allowing the angora to wrap around it and completely cover the core yarn.

8.6 *Spinning around a core.*

8.7 Core yarn, single and plied.

8.8 (below) Novelty yarn spun by Elaine Watkins.

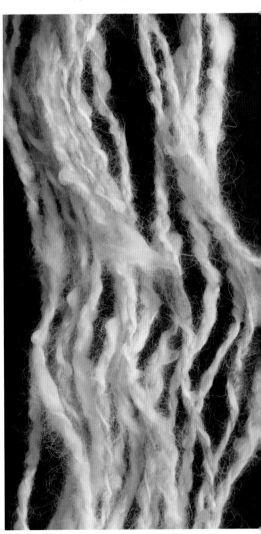

The angora is held almost at right angles to the core. The angora will readily catch on. If you hold both the core yarn and the angora at an equal tension as if you are plying them together, your finished yarn will look like one wool single-plied with an angora single. Our aim is to have a yarn that from the outside looks all angora.

With a little practice, the core will be invisible as it will be surrounded by the angora fibre. Two or three singles of this core yarn can then be plied together or used as a single. Again the true character of the yarn will not show up until it is washed.

NOVELTY YARN

A novelty yarn can be created by spinning a single using the slubs and mats combed from the rabbit's coat and plied with a single ply of angora (see photo 8.8) or silk. (See Chapter 12, pages 189–195 for more on novelty yarns.)

▉ USES

KNITTING

Angora yarn is so soft and light that is makes ideal scarves and shawls. It will be very warm but is not hard-wearing.

WEAVING

I would not recommend this yarn as a weaving yarn in a warp as angora's soft, fluffy texture makes the yarns stick together. However, the core yarn can make an attractive weft yarn for shawls and scarves.

▦ PROJECTS

Booties

Spun & knitted
by Elaine Watkins

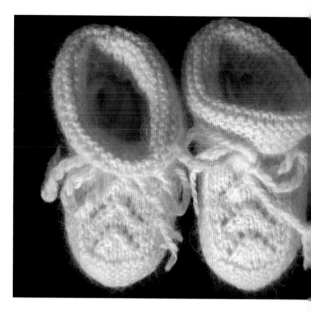

These booties were spun from a mixture of 40% German angora and 60% merino. The pattern came from a Paragon pattern book containing patterns for 21 pairs of bootees, which was published nearly 50 years ago.

Scarf

Spun & woven by Anne Field

This could also be woven on a rigid heddle loom, using pick-up sticks for the pattern areas.

Structure: Plain weave

Equipment: 4 shaft loom, minimum width 23cm (9in) wide, two shuttles. 10 dent reed

Warp and weft yarn: Black 110/3 merino wool (4800 yd/lb)

Pattern weft: 100% angora yarn, spun worsted without any preparation. Used double. Single — 14 wraps per 2.5cm (1in)

Warp length: 3m (9ft) 180 ends

Width in reed: 23cm (9in)

Sett: 20 ends per 2.5cm (1in). 2 per dent in 10 dent reed

Picks per 2.5cm (1in): 20

Weight of finished scarf: 170gm (6oz)

Weaving

Weave in plain weave for 2.5cm, and hemstitch. Weave 5cm (2in) following the surface weave draft in Chapter 1 (see page 35), using the angora yarn doubled. Then weave 10 picks with just the black weft, then 1 pick in the doubled angora again.

Weave for the desired length, and repeat the patten in reverse at the other end. Hemstitch. I hand-washed the scarf in warm, soapy water, rinsed it, and dried it lying flat. Don't press the pattern areas as this will flatten the texture. The borders in the angora yarn could be brushed after washing.

SOURCE: www.nationalangorarabbitbreeders.com

Part Three

PLANT & MANUFACTURED FIBRES

III Plant & manufactured fibres

WHEN ASSESSING FIBRES such as cotton and manufactured fibres, you can use the knowledge you have already gained from your experience of spinning animal fibres. Again informed decisions can be made by observing and handling the fibre before spinning. Hold the fibre up to the light. How long is each fibre? Are the fibres arranged randomly or are they parallel? Are they soft or rough? Are the fibres fine or coarse?

We know that fine fibres spin best into fine yarn, and coarse fibres spin well into thick yarn so the size is virtually decided for us depending on the specific characteristics of the material we are using. Again sample skeins, spun, plied and washed, will give you a lot of information.

New fibres are coming on the market all the time. Tencel (a type of rayon made from wood pulp) and bamboo are just two of these new exciting fibres. Some of these fibres will be randomly dyed into a rainbow of colours, some you can dye yourself before or after spinning. To test the colour changes before and after spinning, take a portion of the fibre, thin it out and give it several twists. Most coloured fibres will darken when they are compressed like this and twisting them together will give you an accurate forecast of what colour the spun yarn will be.

Cotton

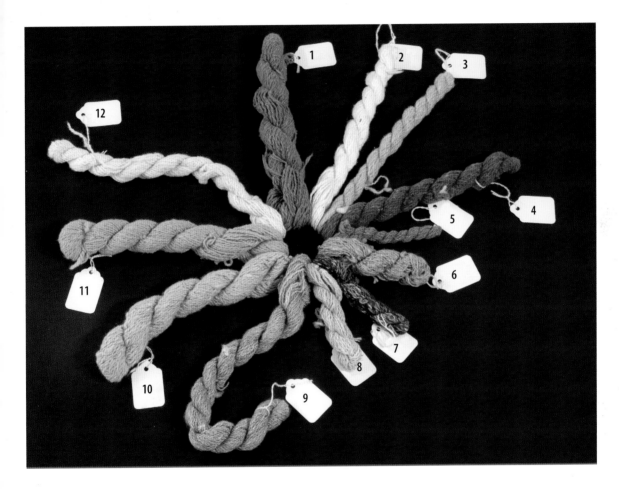

9.1 Sample skeins of cotton yarn spun by Paula Vester. 1. Peruvian cotton; 2. 50/50 cotton/lenzing (a type of rayon); 3. 50/50 brown cotton/tussah silk; 4. Peruvian cotton; 5. Peruvian cotton; 6. recycled blue jean cotton; 7. multi-dyed cotton; 8. cotton/Lyocell/flax; 9. Pima/silk blend; 10. unknown; 11. green cotton/flax; 12. Israeli cotton.

COTTON IS A cellulose, seed-hair fibre and is the most common fibre used in the textile industry all over the world. Microscopically, each cotton fibre is a series of closed tubes containing moisture. The fibre is tightly coiled and these coils straighten out as the seeds ripen, forcing the boll to open. As the air reaches the fibres, the moisture dries out, leaving the fibre flat and ribbon-like with several twists similar to the crimp in wool. These twists make the fibres cling together.

The cotton plant is a shrub and the cotton fibre or boll surrounds and protects the seeds as they ripen and then aids in seed dispersal. About 45–60 days after flowering, the cotton boll bursts open and it is then harvested. It is a tropical plant needing plenty of water and heat as it grows. After harvesting, the bolls are ginned to remove the seeds, and this fibre preparation is called lint.

9.2 Cotton tops.

9.3 (below) Cotton bolls.

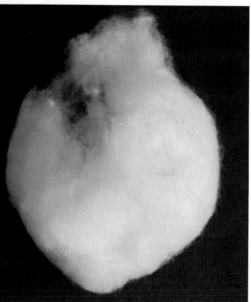

9.4 Cotton lint.

The fibre is then commercially prepared by carding. This process opens and removes any remaining seeds and other vegetable matter. Yarns can be spun from cotton lint and carded cotton sliver, but the fibre can also be combed into top to remove the shorter fibres and make them parallel.

Mercerized cotton, where the fibre is exposed to caustic soda under tension, makes the fibres straighter, stronger and more lustrous, and they dye readily. Mercerized cotton yarn isn't as water-absorbent as unmercerized cotton, so is not suitable for tea towels and bath towels.

Organically grown cotton that has been grown without synthetic agricultural chemicals has become popular with spinners and the cultivation of naturally coloured cotton has become part of this movement. The colours are many and varied and this has made them attractive to spinners.

There are various grades of cotton, mainly judged by length. The finest cotton, Sea Island, has fibres that can be 3.6cm (1½in) long. Egyptian cotton is also long and is softer and more durable than the shorter Pima cotton, a variety of Egyptian cotton, although both are considered to be of high quality. Cotton this long is not common, however. The most common cotton ranges from 2.2cm (7/8in) to 3.3cm (1¼in).

CHARACTERISTICS OF COTTON

- Fine, uniform fibres.
- Resistant to alkalis.
- Weakens with prolonged exposure to sunlight.
- Damaged by mildew.
- Low lustre, unless mercerized.
- Absorbs and releases moisture easily.
- Not damaged by bleach.
- Weakened by acid.
- Strong when wet.
- Low bulk.
- Low static.
- Contains some grease.
- Burns readily, does not self-extinguish and leaves a soft, black ash.

■ SPINNING A YARN TO MATCH THE CHARACTERISTICS

If you are a long-time wool spinner, cotton with its short, slippery fibres seems very different. Adjust your thinking along with your preparation and spinning methods and you will be surprised how well it spins. You can even spin straight from the cotton boll itself. Each boll has seeds surrounded by the cotton fibre. Find the hard seed, separate it from the boll, and gently tug out a circle of fibre.

9.5 Brown and green cotton.

9.6 Spinning from the seed.

9.7 Cotton seeds with the fibre pulled out.

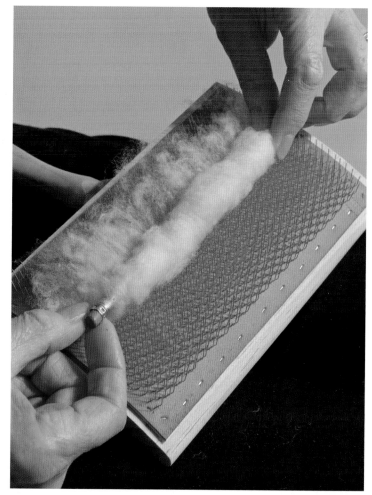

9.8 (above) Carding cotton. Use the same method of carding as described on pages 60–61 but card very lightly keeping the fibre on top of the teeth rather than embedded in them.

9.9 Making a puni. Place the puni stick — a pencil is about the right size — around the fibre at the toe of the carder and roll the fibre around the pencil towards the carder heel. Smooth the puni in your hand but do not compact it. Slide it off the pencil and it is ready to spin.

9.10 (below) Cotton punis.

■ PREPARATION

COMMERCIALLY PREPARED FIBRE

Check to see how it has been prepared. Gently pull apart a narrow section of the fibre. If the fibres are parallel and the same length, you have combed tops (see photo 9.2, page 154). If the fibres break apart unevenly and are randomly arranged, you have carded fibre (see photo 9.4, page 154).

The combed preparation will seem more slippery to spin, as the parallel fibres will readily move past one another. The yarn will be smoother and denser. The carded preparation will produce a yarn that is lighter and less dense.

PREPARING THE FIBRE YOURSELF

Because the fibres are short, a type of rolag preparation called a puni is useful. Try to use fine hand carders to card the cotton fibre. Specially made cotton carders can have 200 points per square inch (ppsi). If you have wool carders, the finer 108 ppsi can be used.

SPINNING

Traditionally cotton was spun on a charkha wheel, made famous by Gandhi when he attempted to revive the India cotton industry (see page 18 for a charkha wheel). Great wheels were also used for spinning cotton (see page 18).

The best treadle wheels are those with a high drive ratio as cotton needs more twist than wool. A drive ratio of 10 upwards will let you put in the required amount of twist without having to treadle quickly. Flyer-led wheels are easier for cotton spinning as you can have a looser tension on the brake band than the drive band.

If you are an inexperienced medium or long-draw spinner, first try spinning cotton with a modified short forward or backward draft. Spinning from a puni rather than from prepared carded or combed cotton gives the fibre some cohesion which will help if this is your first try at cotton spinning. Spinning from carded cotton also helps as the random arrangement of the fibres also adds cohesion, but not as much as the puni preparation. Combed top is slippery and may fly through your hands before you have even thought about drafting!

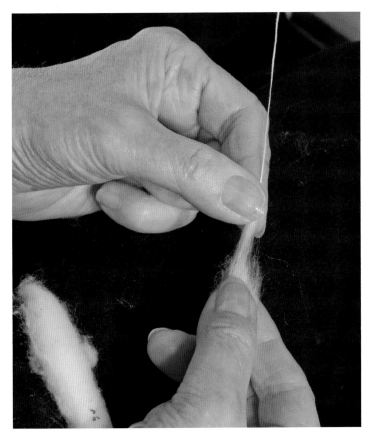

9.11 Reduce the tension on the brake band so the flyer is just turning. You should feel very little pull on the leader. The front and back hand must be kept close together as the cotton fibre is so short. Keep the twist just ahead of the front hand.

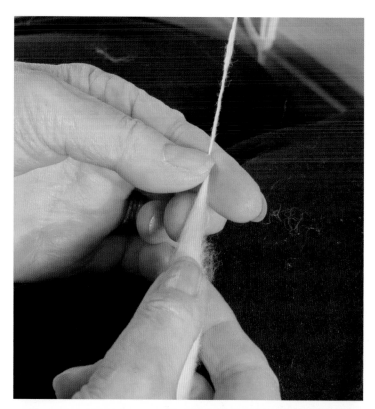

9.12 You can use the thumb and forefinger of your front hand in a rolling movement to either open or close the twist.

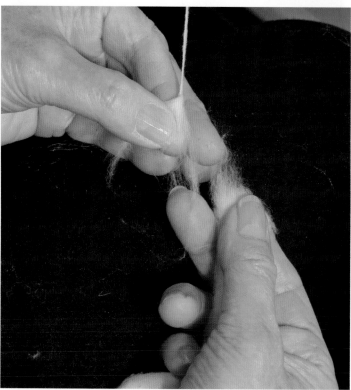

9.13 Join a new fibre supply as you would with wool (see page 27), making sure you are overlapping and joining two fluffy, untwisted ends.

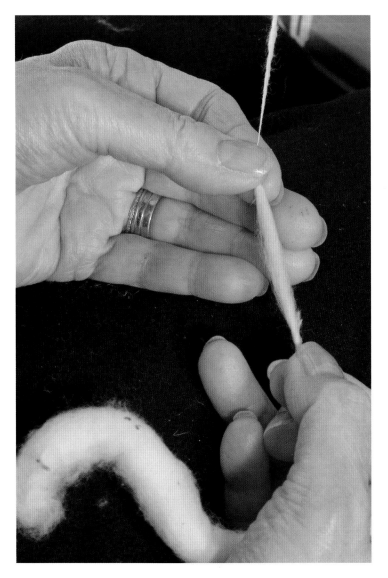

9.14 Don't leave long, fluffy slubs in the yarn. These are weak areas and will rub and break later. Stop spinning and gently pull these areas apart while untwisting the yarn.

SPINNING WITH THE MEDIUM OR LONG DRAW (see pages 65–67)
Many spinners advocate this method of spinning as the only way to spin the short cotton fibres. There are many different methods of spinning so try different ones until you find the one that suits you best.

Again you may find punis easier to begin with, but also try spinning with carded or combed cotton. The combed cotton will give you the smoothest, slightly denser yarn but will feel slippery. Again the tension on the brake band should be light.

▨ PLYING

Let the yarn sit on the bobbins overnight as it will set and be easier to ply. You can use single yarn on its own, ply with another cotton single or ply it with another stronger thread such as sewing cotton.

Problem solving

- The fibres keep breaking in the drafting zone.
  Solution: Your hands are too far apart. Compared to spinning wool, your hands will hardly seem to move apart at all.
- The yarn is over-twisted and kinks and curls and won't pull onto the bobbin.
  Solution: The tension on the brake band may be too loose or your hands and feet are not working in unison. Try treadling more slowly or drafting more quickly.
- The fibre will not pull out easily from the puni.
  Solution: The puni may be too solid, with either too much fibre in one puni or you may have squashed the puni when smoothing it down. Make a smaller puni with a lighter hand.

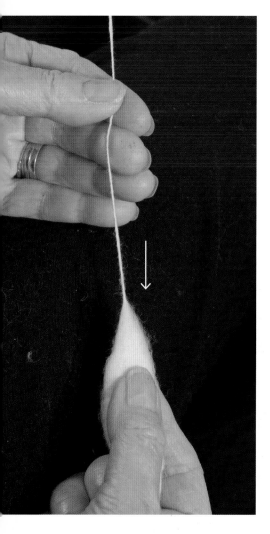

9.15 Medium draft. Let plenty of twist accumulate before you draft back.

Problem solving

- The fibre breaks in the drafting area.
  Solution: Let more twist into the drafting area before you draft back.

 WASHING

Again there are several methods of washing the yarn. Try each one to see which you prefer because different methods will suit different finished projects.

BOILING
If the finished article will be subject to heavy wear, this is a good method that will strengthen the yarn. The skeins can be tied, then put with water in the microwave until the water boils. If you are dyeing the finished yarn, the oils that are present in the cotton, although not noticeable, will prevent complete absorption of the dye stuff. In this case boil the yarn for at least two hours to scour it. Add 1 teaspoon of detergent to 3.8 litres (1 gallon) of water and 60gm (2oz) of washing soda per 28gm (1oz) of yarn.

WASHING IN HOT WATER
If the yarn will not be subjected to heavy wear, washing in hot, soapy water is adequate.

 USES
KNITTING

You can use cotton for the same projects as wool, e.g., hats, scarves, jerseys, etc. However, if you are a beginning cotton spinner, start with small projects such as a hat, mittens or a very small scarf.

WEAVING

An experienced cotton spinner can use handspun cotton for a warp. Usually it is sized first with laundry starch. It can be used as a weft without sizing. For your first weaving project, I suggest you use a commercially spun cotton warp and a handspun weft. If you use a mercerized cotton for the warp, it will add lustre but will not be as absorbent as the handspun cotton.

■ **PROJECTS**

Child's beret
Crocheted by Paula Vester

As Paula is such a good crocheter, she makes up her pattern as she goes. This beret was begun in the top centre and increased in the traditional way every other row (2sc in each previous st, then sc, 2sc, then sc, sc, 2sc, and so on — Paula used US crochet terms) until it was the right size. The stitches were then doubled to make the part that puffed out and the bobble stitch was interspaced about the middle of the enlarged section. After a few more rows, Paula decreased to fit the head, then crocheted a few more rows to make the bottom edge straight, as the beret was worked in a spiral.

9.16 Child's beret spun and crocheted.

161

Small cardigan
Spun & knitted by Anne Field

The cotton I spun for this teddy bear cardigan was 18 wraps per 2.5cm and I used size 3.25mm (US 3, UK 10) needles. This fitted the teddy bear in the photograph opposite which was 20cm (8in) high. The cardigan weighed 11gm (½ oz). Even although this cardigan was so small and you may not want to knit clothes for teddy bears, it is a very useful pattern, showing how to knit from the top down. The pattern is from *A Beginner's Guide to Knitting from the Top Down* by Leslie Bronson, Cartersville, GA, USA, and is used here with her kind permission.

Teddy bear cardigan with raglan sleeves
This pattern will fit a teddy bear or doll about 18 inches tall if the yarn is US worsted weight (3500 yards per pound), 11–12 wraps per 2.5cm (1in).

Abbreviations
K = knit
P = purl
yo = yarn over
* * = repeat

Materials needed
Several gm (oz) of yarn
Knitting needles, size 5.5mm (US 8, UK 5)
Double-pointed needles, size 5.5mm (US 8, UK 5) (optional)
Crochet hook for edging, size 4.5mm (US G) (optional)
Tapestry needle to weave in loose ends
2 stitch holders or contrasting yarn
4 or 5 stitch markers or extra yarn tied in loops
Note: you can substitute a chunky yarn and 7.5mm, (US 11, UK 1) needles to make a cardigan large enough to fit a three-month-old baby.

Knitting the sweater's yoke
Beginning at the neck, cast on 32 sts.
Row 1: P across.
Row 2: K4, place marker, *K8, place marker* 3 times, K4.
Row 3: P across.
Row 4: K3, yo, *K2, yo, K6, yo* 3 times, K2, yo, K3 (40 sts).
Row 5: P across.
Row 6: K4, yo, *K2, yo, K8, yo* 3 times, K2, yo, K4 (48 sts).
Row 7: P across.
Row 8: K5, yo, *K2, yo, K10, yo* 3 times, K2, yo, K5 (56 sts).
Row 9: P across.

9.17 A very small cardigan.

Row 10: K6, yo, *K2, yo, K12, yo* 3 times, K2, yo, K6 (64 sts).
Row 11: P across.
Row 12: K7, yo, *K2, yo, K14, yo* 3 times, K2, yo, K7 (72 sts).
Row 13: P across.
Row 14: K8, yo, *K2, yo, K16, yo* 3 times, K2, yo, K8 (80 sts).
Row 15: P across.
Row 16: K10, remove markers as you come to them, place 20 sts on holder, K20, place 20 sts on holder, K10 (40 sts on needle).
You should now have 40 sts for the body of the sweater on your needle, and two sleeves (20 sts each) on stitch holders.

Knitting the sweater's body
Row 17: Continue in stocking stitch pattern for 12 rows (40 sts). Cast off.

Knitting the sweater's sleeves
Pick up 20 sts off one stitch holder. Knit in stocking stitch for 10 rows. Cast off.
Use double-pointed needles to knit the sleeve in the round with no seam, or knit the sleeve back and forth on the on straight needles and sew up the sleeve seam.
Repeat with last 20 sts to make the second sleeve.
Add a row of single crochet along the cardigan's edges, if desired.
Weave in loose yarn ends, block and you're finished!

Manufactured fibres

THERE ARE TWO different types of manufactured fibre: the most common are man-made from natural sources. This group includes fibres such as Lyocell and bamboo manufactured from regenerated cellulose, and regenerated protein fibre, such as soy and corn. The other group of manufactured fibres has a chemical base, such as nylon and acrylics. As spinners we are mostly interested in the first group.

Spinners generally buy these fibres in commercially prepared forms. Slowly pull apart the preparation to gauge the fibre length and strength.

10.1 Bamboo in its natural state.

CELLULOSE FIBRES

This is fibre from plant material that has been pulped, then goes through various processes to form a viscose solution which is forced through a spinneret to form filaments of thread. The resulting thread is rayon, regardless of the type of process, or the original source, whether it is bamboo or Lyocell (commonly called Tencel).

Rayon has been around for a long time as it was first made in the 1880s. It was first called artificial silk as this is what it resembled. In the 1920s the name was changed to rayon and this is still the correct term for all regenerated cellulose fibre.

10.2 Tencel fibre and spun yarn.

CHARACTERISTICS OF LYOCELL

- Wrinkle resistant.
- Excellent drape and handle.
- Lustrous.
- Absorbent.
- Dyes easily, with the same dyes used for cotton.
- Strong when wet.
- No elasticity.
- Slippery.
- Burns readily, does not shrink from the flame and leaves a black or grey ash.
- Biodegradable.
- Soft.
- Little shrinkage.

LYOCELL (TENCEL)

This is a fibre made from wood pulp. SeaCell is another Lyocell fibre that includes seaweed. Lyocell was first sold to the public in 1991 so it is a relatively new fibre. To form thread, the chemically processed pulp is pumped through a spinneret, rather like water through a shower-head. Most of the waste and chemicals are recycled. The thread, called tow, is then carded after which it can be spun into yarn on its own or mixed with other fibres such as cotton or wool.

Spinning

Spin as for silk (see pages 119–120).

10.3 Bamboo fibre and spun yarn.

BAMBOO

This is actually a grass, not a tree, although it can grow very tall. It is considered an easily renewable source of fibre as the plant is very quick growing, doesn't require replanting and usually doesn't require the use of pesticides and herbicides to thrive. The fibre structure contains minute air pockets that let the fibre absorb moisture well.

Bamboo fibre for spinning can be produced in the same way as Lyocell; that is, the pulp undergoes a chemical process, is pumped through a spinneret and then carded. This is the most common process, but traditionally bamboo was retted and treated like flax. This process can now be done commercially and, although not common, this fibre is available.

Spinning

Spin as for silk (see pages 119–120).

CHARACTERISTICS OF BAMBOO

- High antibacterial and antifungal qualities.
- High water absorbency, can take up to three times its weight in water.
- Drapes well.
- Cool to wear.
- Soft.
- Smooth.
- Lustrous.
- Good insulating properties.
- Dyes well.

10.4 Soy fibre and yarn spun by Pauline Pease.

CHARACTERISTICS OF SOY FIBRE

- Lustrous.
- Soft and warm.
- Smooth.
- Drapes well.
- Dyes easily.
- Biodegradable.
- Antibacterial.
- Very slippery.
- Same moisture absorbency as cotton.
- Little shrinkage.
- Strong.
- Crease resistant.
- No elasticity.
- Will fuzz up but not pill.

◼ REGENERATED PROTEIN FIBRES

SOY FIBRE

Soy fibre was first made in the 1930s and was redeveloped in the 1990s. The fibre is made from soy oil from soybean cake and is naturally a gold colour, similar to tussah silk, but it can be bleached white. The manufacturing process is similar to that of the rayons, with the processed protein passed through a spinneret.

Spinning

Spin as for silk but with more twist because it is a very slippery fibre.

SYNTHETIC FIBRES

These are chemically based.

NYLON

This is the most common synthetic fibre from a family of synthetic polymers known generically as polyamides. It was first produced in the late 1930s and was intended to be a synthetic replacement for silk. It can be made from coal, natural gas or petroleum.

Spinning

This fibre is often mixed with other fibres to give it more strength, as in sock-knitting yarns, and usually is not spun on its own. It also makes a good core or wrap yarn as it is so strong. However, because it is so slippery, when used as a core yarn, e.g., with angora, nylon will not grip the fibre as well as a wool core yarn.

10.5 The characteristics of nylon mean that it is also ideal for making rope.

CHARACTERISTICS OF NYLON

- Similar to wool in structure.
- Takes wool dyes and has superior colour fastness.
- Very strong.
- Melts when burnt and will burn rapidly after it melts. Shrinks from the flame. Self-extinguishing.
- Resists abrasion.
- Has elasticity.
- Crease resistant but pleats and creases can be set at high temperatures.
- Low absorbency.
- Contains static electricity.
- Strong when wet.
- Resistant to mould and mildew and many chemicals.
- Lightweight.
- Slippery.

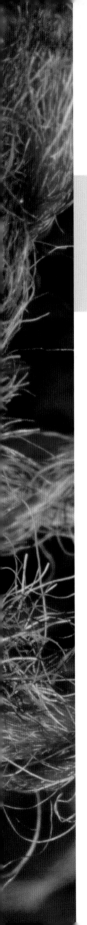

Part Four

MIXING & MATCHING FIBRES

IV Mixing & matching fibres

IN THIS SECTION of the book, many of the skills learnt in earlier chapters will be used. You will now have the skills to mix different fibres together: you are able to look at individual fibres, decide on the properties you want in the finished yarn, then choose the proportions of each. And always remember to sample!

If you apply this knowledge to the making of novelty yarns, you will find that the possibilities are endless and that your spinning world will expand enormously. Could I incorporate those seeds into my yarn? What happens if I unravel that old jersey and re-spin it with some beads added? What happens if I ply some commercial pre-shrunk wool with some high-shrink merino? You will be amazed at what you can come up with.

Blended fibres

11

AS THE RANGE of spinning fibres increase, so do the ways we can mix them together. Sometimes the number of blended fibres we can spin is bewildering. Fibres can be mixed so one predominates over the other, we can blend equal amounts of each, or we can add just a touch of some luxurious and expensive fibre. Sometimes the fibres are too short to be used on their own, as is the possum fibre we will discuss later in this chapter. The addition of a fine, crimpy wool adds length and elasticity to the possum fibre and makes it easy to spin.

11.1 Commercially prepared carded alpaca/silk fibre and spun yarn.

11.2 Hat spun by Anne Field; dyed and modelled by grand-daughter Larissa Field (with some encouragement) and knitted by her proud grandmother.

175

Checking blended fibres

Another point to note when buying fibres that have been commercially blended is to see which way they are blended. Are they carded into a random preparation suitable for woollen (see page 64) or semi-worsted (see page 58) spinning, or is the preparation made of parallel fibres suitable for worsted (see page 52) or semi-woollen spinning (see page 68)? Pull the prepared fibres apart to see how they are aligned (see page 54).

If we buy the fibres already blended, most of these are clearly marked with the proportion of each, e.g., 60% merino, 40% Tencel. Therefore, if we know the properties of each of the components as outlined in the previous chapters, we can understand what to use these blends for and how to spin them. As an example, a blend of merino/Tencel will have the softness of both of these fibres, the Tencel will add lustre, and the wool will add elasticity and give some grab to the fibre when spinning. And we know from the information that the fibres are almost equal, using slightly more wool than Tencel. A blend of 75% wool and 25% Tencel will have more of the characteristics of wool as that is the main component.

Blended fibres, whether commercially prepared or prepared by ourselves, can be completely mixed together so there is no trace of each individual component. The other way is to partially mix the different fibres so each individual component is still seen. A silk/cashmere blend I spun still had streaks of the silk gleaming through the dull cashmere, and these streaks remained in the finished yarn.

It's fun to mix our own fibres and there are two ways of doing this. We can mix the fibres on hand or drum carders or mini-combs and then spin them, or we can spin one fibre and then ply that with a single of another fibre. In this chapter we will discuss these options.

▮ COMMERCIALLY PREPARED FIBRE

ALPACA/SILK (See photos 11.1 & 11.2, page 175)

This fibre is 30% silk and 70% alpaca. As the preparation was carded, the fibres were randomly arranged. The silk was completely blended in with the alpaca. I spun it using the short forward draft (a worsted spin), so the finished yarn was semi-worsted. It was a joy to spin. The silk gave the yarn some lustre and added to the softness. The yarn size after washing was 20 wraps per 2.5cm (1in). The pattern was based on the basic hat pattern on page 75 and was knitted on size 3.25mm (US 3, UK 10) needles.

WHEN I WAS a child I made lots of pom-poms. I can't remember using them for anything but they were fun to make. I used milk-bottle tops, which had a hole punched out to put a straw into. When I made the pom-pom for Larissa's hat (page 175), I found I could still remember how to make them, although I had to use cut-up cardboard instead of milk-bottle tops.

Cut two circles of firm card with a smaller circular hole cut out of the centre (like a doughnut). Put the two circles together, then wind yarn around and around the two circles from the inner to the outer circle. The bigger the cardboard circles, the bigger the pom-pom. When you have done enough layers, cut the wool between the edges of the two cardboard circles with sharp, pointed scissors. Hold on to the circles firmly so the cut ends don't slide off. Still holding the circles, ease them slightly apart, wind a length of wool tightly between the two now separated circles, wind it around a couple of times, then tie a knot to hold it. This tie binds the cut wool strands together. Slide off the two cardboard circles and you have your pom-pom. There are good instructions for making pom-poms on websites on the Internet.

POSSUM/MERINO

This is a yarn unique to New Zealand. We have millions of possums and they are a real pest. Possums are marsupials and were brought into New Zealand from Australia in the 1800s to start up a fur trade. Because New Zealand has no natural predators, they multiply rapidly and the destruction they cause in our forests is alarming. Using this yarn has turned a pest, that every effort has been made to eradicate, into a useful provider of a unique, much-prized yarn.

The fibre length is very short — about 2–3cm (1–1¼in) is the norm.

11.3 (left) New Zealand possum.

11.4 (above) Possum fur.

11.5 (below) Possum/merino fibre (70% merino, 30% possum fur).

11.6 (below left) Possum/merino yarn, spun woollen from commercially prepared carded fibre.

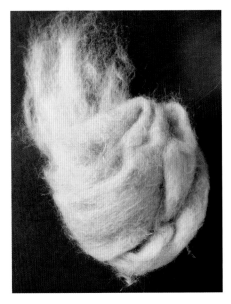

177

The fur can be plucked or shorn, the plucked fur being longer and less likely to shed from the finished yarn. Winter fur is also longer and thicker than the summer coat. The fur fibre is hollow and very light, so garments made from this blend weigh very little.

Because the fur fibre is so short, it needs to be mixed with something to give it length; merino is ideal because it is the softest wool and very elastic. The possum fur gives the yarn a halo effect which is apparent when the yarn has been washed.

MERINO/SILK BLEND

This yarn was a blend of 80% combed merino and 20% silk. I spun it woollen, to make a bouncy, soft, semi-woollen yarn.

MOHAIR/CORRIEDALE BLEND

This fibre was a carded blend of 60% Corriedale and 40% mohair. This yarn was also spun woollen. As I am mainly a weaver, not a knitter, I usually spin my yarns worsted, so spinning these last two blends has been good practice for me.

11.7 Mohair/Corriedale fibre and yarn sample.

11.8 Merino/silk fibre and yarn sample.

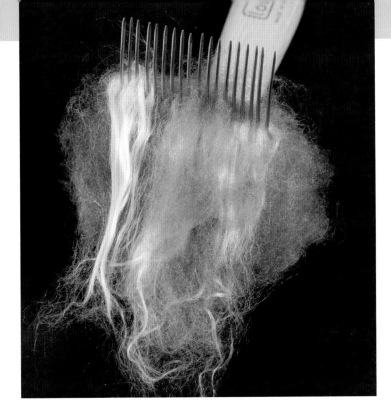

11.9 On the comb, lay in two layers of carded Romney wool, one layer of silk tops, then two layers of the wool again. Only one comb was used, as the fibres weren't transferred from one comb to the other.

11.10 (below) Using a diz (see page 55), the fibre was removed from the comb.

11.11 (bottom) Worsted-spun skein of wool and silk.

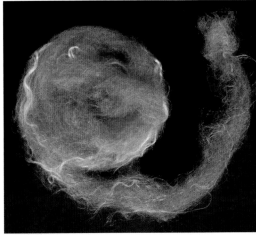

BLENDING YOUR OWN FIBRES

Doing the blending yourself gives you complete freedom as you can choose the fibres, the amounts of each and the blending method. If you have a lot of fibre to prepare, use a drum carder. For smaller amounts, hand carders are useful. Remember that hand and drum carders prepare wool so it lies in a random arrangement suitable for woollen or semi-worsted spinning. If you want to spin a worsted or semi-woollen yarn, the fibres can be blended on mini-combs.

If you want a uniform blend, weigh out the components each time before you start so you get enough fibre with the same quantities of each of the components. If you want the fibres to be completely blended together, make several passes through the combs, hand or drum carders.

BLENDING FIBRES ON MINI-COMBS

For a fluffier yarn I could have woollen-spun this sample skein. The amount of each fibre can vary. If you want the fibres to be completely blended use both combs to transfer the fibres a couple of times from one comb to the other. For the sample in photo 11.9, I wanted streaks of silk to show through the carded wool, so I did not transfer the fibre to the second comb. You can also use locks of wool, mohair or alpaca on the combs to blend with other fibres. Try to choose fibres that are the same length.

11.12 Lay silk and wool on one carder. For this sample I used washed Polwarth wool and silk. The silk was cut to the same length as the Polwarth locks. It took several passes of the carders to blend the fibres.

11.13 (below) Woollen-spun skein of Polwarth wool and silk.

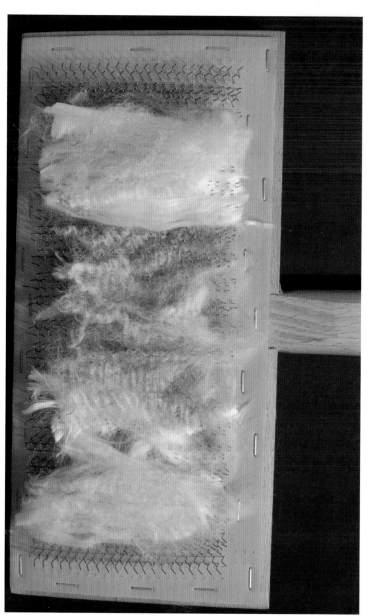

BLENDING ON HAND CARDERS

When blending on hand carders, it is easier to chose fibres that are the same length, but the proportions can vary. For example, you can card 10% silk and 90% wool to add more lustre to the wool. If you want the fibres to be completely blended, make several passes of the fibre from one carder to the other. To spin a yarn that has streaks of one fibre through the other, make fewer passes.

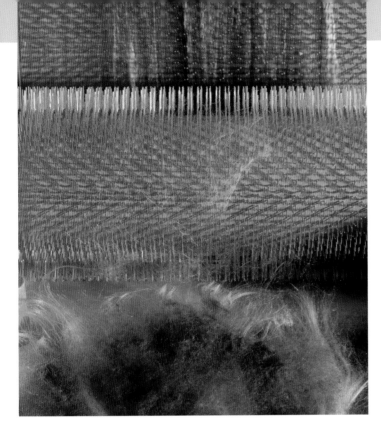

11.14 Place a thin layer of opened locks on the tray, then spread a thin layer of silk, then another layer of locks. Pull the silk apart rather than cutting it, as short fibres will catch on the small drum. For this sample I used Romney fleece and bombyx silk.

11.15 (below) If too much of the silk ends up on the small drum, the silk fibres can be added directly to the large drum.

BLENDING ON A DRUM CARDER

If you are blending a very short fibre, such as possum or cotton, with wool on the drum carder, make a batt of wool first on the drum carder. Then fold the batt over the possum fibres, break up the batt into smaller portions and feed this through the carder, repeating this process once or twice. If you try to add the possum to the wool staples before you put them both through the drum carder, the short fibres will collect on the small drum.

11.16 Batt of silk and wool after two passes through the drum carder.

11.17 Silk single and Corriedale sliver single plied together.

PLYING TWO DIFFERENT YARNS TOGETHER

It is helpful to know the characteristics of each fibre beforehand. If you ply a very shrinkable single with a non-shrinkable single, you can get interesting novelty yarn. For example, when plying one strand of merino with a strand of Tencel, the merino will shrink, the Tencel won't and you end up with an interesting, textured yarn. (See Chapter 12, pages 189–195 for more novelty yarns.) If this was intentional, this is fine, but if it is accidental it is irritating. Using a shrink-proof merino fibre will make for a smoother yarn.

A shiny yarn plied with a dull yarn will have a different appearance to two dull yarns plied together. Two very different colours and types of fibre will produce a striking and exciting yarn, whereas similar colours will produce a harmonious yarn. There are a lot of factors to consider. Another point is that a fluffy, open arrangement of fibres will darken when it is solidified into yarn. I have chosen a bag of prepared sliver because I loved the colour only to find it changed considerably when I spun it into yarn. To test colours, I twist some of the fibres with my fingers in an approximation of what the yarn will look like when spun.

BRUSHING THE FINISHED GARMENT

With some blends the surface can be brushed after knitting or weaving to bring up the pile. The hand-carded blend below (11.18a) is merino top (60%), angora rabbit (30%), white and green silk (9%) and green glitz or angelina (1% approx.). Sue Giller spun the yarn semi-worsted. The finished garment was brushed with a teasel.

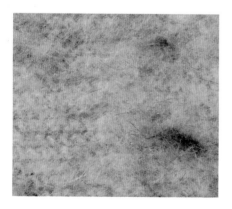

11.18a & b A hand-carded blend of merino top, angora rabbit, white and green silk and green glitz (right). The finished garment, a shoulder warmer, was brushed with a teasel to bring up the pile (above).

PROJECTS

Scarf
Spun & knitted by Rosalind Thomson

Two singles, one of handspun merino and one of handspun silk, were plied together. The silk single was tightly twisted so it would hold together. The scarf was knitted on jumbo needles, 5cm (2in) in circumference. The finished scarf looks as if beads were added as the silk gleams and glitters against the wool.

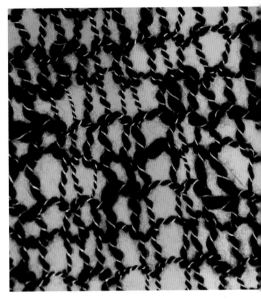

11.19 Knitted scarf (with detail, above).

Spinning-wheel shawl
Spun & knitted by Lyn Hodge, Australia

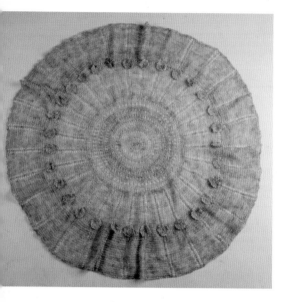

Abbreviations

psso = pass slipped st over
sc = single crochet chain (English
  terms used)
sl = slip
st/s = stitch/es
tog = together
y fwd = yarn forward

Spinning-wheel shawl pattern

Elizabeth Zimmerman's well-known P1 construction used courtesy of Schoolhouse Press, with thanks to Meg and Michelle.

Materials used

Gotland fleece from Megan Philip, Martinborough, New Zealand.
Spun singles 5–6 twists per 2.5cm (1in) and 20 wraps per 2.5cm
  (1in). Plied with silk singles to make a 4–5 ply balanced yarn.
Circular needles: 5mm and 6mm (US 7–9, UK 6–4).
Double-pointed needles: 1 set size 4mm (US 5, UK 8). The tension
  (gauge) is not important when knitting this pattern as the size
  is not critical. So choose the needle size that is suitable for your
  yarn size.
Diameter: 118cms (47in)

Method

Single crochet 4 sts. Join with slip stitch.
Make 9sc in the circle. Pick up the 9 single crochet sts and place
  them on 3 double-point needles (3 sts on each needle).
Knit 1 round.
Note: The rounds between holes were worked with knit 1 round,
  purl 1 round for the number of rounds required.
Next round: *yarn over K1 rep from *(18 sts). Knit 3 rounds.
Next round: *yarn over K1 rep from *(36 sts). Knit 6 rounds.
Next round: *yarn over K1 rep from *(72 sts).
Change to 5mm circular needle.
Knit 12 rounds adding Elizabeth Zimmerman's method of an
  imitation increase round on the sixth row of: yarn over, K2 tog.
Next round: *yarn over K1 rep from *(144 sts).
Knit 24 rounds.
Sixth round: *yarn over K2 tog rep from *.
Twelfth round: *yarn over K2 tog rep from *.
Eighteenth round: *yarn over K2 rep from *.
Next round: yarn over K1 rep from *(288 sts).
Knit 48 rounds in Pattern 1.

11.20 Spinning-wheel shawl.

Pattern 1
Round 1: *K6 sts y fwd sl 1 K2 tog psso rep from *.
Round 2: *P6 sts K3 sts rep from *.
Next round: *yarn over K1 rep from *(576 sts).
Change to 6mm circular needle and work 40 rounds in pattern 2.

Pattern 2
Round 1: *K15 sts y fwd sl 1 K2 tog psso rep from *.
Round 2: *P15 sts K3 sts rep from *.
Cast off.

Crochet wheels (English terms used)
Ch 4 join with a sl st.
Ch 1 12 sc in circle.
Ch 2 1 sc in same space Ch 2 *1 sc in next sc Ch 2 rep from *.
Ch 4 1 sc in same space* Ch 4 1 sc in next 1 Ch space rep from *.
Fasten off.

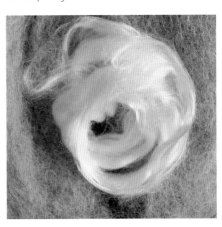

11.21 Gotland fleece, washed and carded, and silk sliver.

Child's beanie
Spun & knitted by Chris Eves

Materials used

Hand-dyed, super angorino tops in blues, greys and white (18 micron merino and 10% angora, from Ixchel; see source list at end of chapter) with a little extra angora in grey and white from Wombat the rabbit, added by Chris.

Wraps per 2.5cm (1in): 15

Size: 2/3 yrs 50cm (20in) circumference

Rib: 5cm (2in) to fold over at 2.5cm

Tension: 25 sts per 10cm (4in) and 38 rows per 10cm (4in)

Decreases: = 6 sts on each decrease round

Needles: 3.25mm (US 3, UK 10) dpns (double-pointed needles) or circulars (although dpns will be needed closer to the crown.) 3.5mm (US 4, UK 9)

Pattern

Using 3.25mm dpns or circulars cast on 120 sts.

Knit 10cms (4in) rib : K1, P1 then place a marker to indicate start of round.

Change to 3.5mm needles and begin Row 1. Use stocking stitch for all rounds.

Rows 1 and 2: Knit — no shaping.

Row 3: Decrease 6 sts evenly across the round and place marker at each decrease.

Rows 4 and 5: Knit — no shaping.

Row 6: Decrease 6 sts evenly across the round, one stitch at each marker.

Rows 7 and 8: Knit — no shaping.

Row 9: Decrease 6 sts evenly across the round, one stitch at each marker.

Row 10: Knit — no shaping.

Row 11: Decrease 6 sts evenly across the round, one stitch at each marker.

Row 12: Knit — no shaping.

Row 13: Decrease 6 sts evenly across the round, one stitch at each marker.

Rows 14 and 15: Knit — no shaping.

Row 16: Decrease 6 sts evenly across the round, one stitch at each marker.

Rows 17 and 18: Knit — no shaping.

Row 19: Decrease 6 sts evenly across the round, one stitch at each marker.

Rows 20, 21 and 22: Knit — no shaping.

Row 23: Decrease 6 sts evenly across the round, one stitch at each marker.

Rows 24 and 25: Knit — no shaping.

Row 26: Decrease 6 sts evenly across the round, one stitch at each marker.

Row 27: Knit — no shaping.

Row 28: Decrease 6 sts evenly across the round, one stitch at each marker.

Row 29: Knit — no shaping

Row 30: Decrease 6 sts evenly across the round, one stitch at each marker.

Row 31: Knit — no shaping

11.22 Beanie (left) and spun yarn (above).

Row 32: Decrease 6 sts evenly across the round, one stitch at each marker.

Row 33: Knit — no shaping

Row 34: Decrease 6 sts evenly across the round, one stitch at each marker.

Rows 35, 36, 37, 38, 39, 40: Decrease 6 sts evenly across the round, one stitch at each marker.

Row 41: Decrease 2 sts evenly.

Making icord

Place the remaining 4 sts on one needle and knit 4 rounds as an icord. To do this have all stitches on one dpn and knit a row. Then zoom all the stitches to the right end of the needle. The yarn will now be at the back of the row (to the left of all the stitches). Pull the yarn to the right hand end so that it sits ready for knitting. The yarn will be at the back and the cord will be facing the front. Commence the next row of knit stitch. Continue in this way until the desired length is achieved. In this hat the icord is about 4 rows long. It could be made longer and then tweaked into a curl to make it a koru (Maori word meaning new life).

Sew ends in and put on a little person.

SOURCES

Gotland from Megan Philip, Martinborough, New Zealand, ruakokopatuna@hotmail.com

Ixchel is an Australian fibre farm which breeds angora rabbits, pesticide-free.

Camelid fibres, cashmere, mohair and merino are also available: Ixchelbunny.blogspot.com

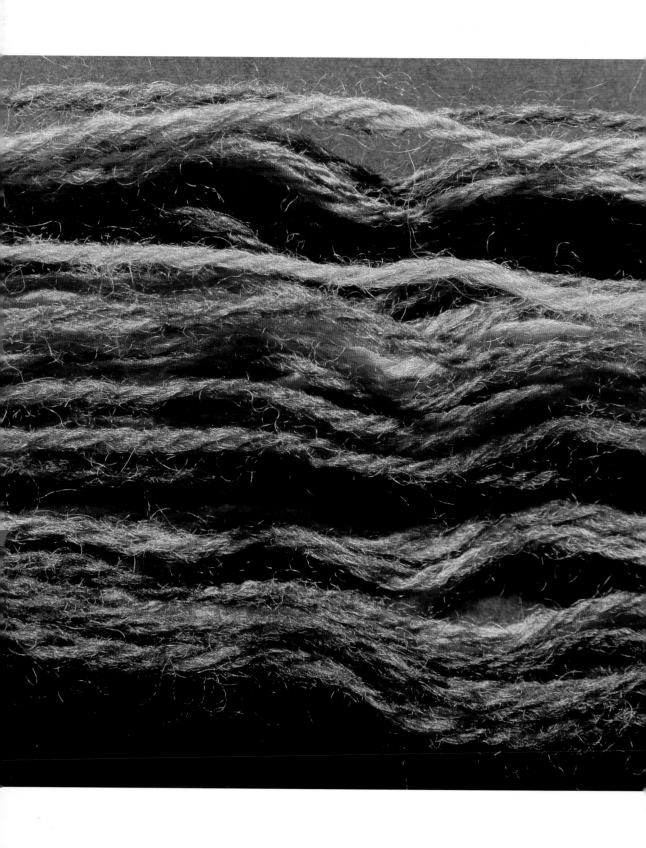

Novelty yarns

12

NOVELTY YARNS are fun to play with and even a small amount added to a knitted or woven fabric can add excitement and glamour to your work. Most of these yarns are best used as a weft for woven cloth as the texture may stop the yarn from moving easily through the heddle eyes on the loom. With most of these yarns, it will help the plying if the handspun singles are left on the bobbins overnight to stabilise them.

SPINNING LUMPY, BUMPY YARN ON PURPOSE

A correctly spun and plied yarn will be rounded with a definite twist (see photo 1.34A, page 29). It will be consistent in size throughout the length. However, there are many times we want more textured yarn. If you are a real beginner, you will have no trouble as this is just the type of yarn you are producing. Weavers love it. Texture is a nice way of saying that your yarn is lumpy! To spin a stable, lumpy yarn, it is best to make your yarn one size throughout, but with lumps added, as in Fig. 7.

If the yarn has thick and thin places, there will be lots of twist in the thin areas and very little in the thick areas (7A). Thin sections need more twist to make the yarn stronger, but too much twist weakens it. Conversely, thick places are strong enough without much twist but will fluff up with wear. By spinning an even base yarn, then adding bumps at intervals, the yarn has an interesting texture without losing strength (7B). To add bumps, pinch the fibre behind the place where the twisted yarn meets the untwisted yarn.

12.1 Textured yarn.

12.2 Making lumps on purpose.

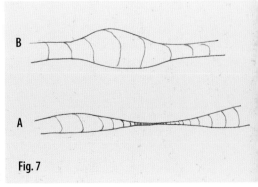

B

A

Fig. 7

SPIRAL YARN

This is a quick way to make a textured yarn as one strand is a commercial cotton or wool. Spin a light, fluffy, thick single woollen yarn with a Z twist (the wheel is turning clockwise).

Place this bobbin of woollen-spun yarn on the lazy kate. I used a cotton sewing thread for the other core yarn, so this spool is added to the lazy kate as well.

There are two ways of plying these two yarns: photo 12.3 plain spiral yarn, or photos 12.4 and 12.5, wrapped spiral yarn.

To stabilise the yarn, wash in very hot water, agitate it for a while, then put the skein straight into a cold rinse. This will slightly felt the yarn.

A fine wool, either handspun or a commercial yarn, can be substituted for the cotton sewing thread.

12.3 (above) Plain spiral yarn; alpaca and cotton. Ply as normal S twist (wheel turning anticlockwise) with equal tension on both the cotton and the alpaca singles.

12.4 (above right) Wrapped spiral yarn; alpaca and cotton.

12.5 Ply the single and the cotton sewing thread together with the wheel turning anticlockwise (S twist). Hold the core yarn under tension in one hand while holding the woollen-spun yarn loosely in the other hand at right angles to the core yarn. The soft woollen-spun yarn wraps itself around the cotton core yarn.

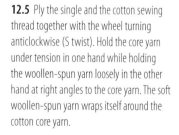

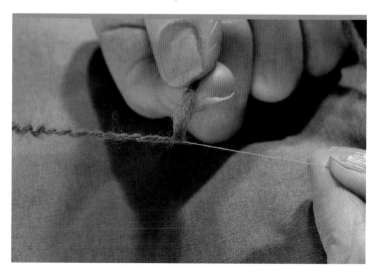

BOUCLÉ YARN

Spin a woollen or worsted yarn with a Z twist (clockwise), more even than the singles in photos 12.3, 12.4 and 12.5. Place this single bobbin on the lazy kate, again with a spool of cotton sewing thread.

The yarn can be stabilised by washing, as with the spiral yarn, or it can be plied with a third binder yarn to add stability. To add the binder, put the bobbin of bouclé yarn onto a lazy kate. The binder yarn (a fine wool or cotton commercial yarn) on a cone or a ball, sits on the floor. Ply the two together Z (clockwise).

12.6 (above) Bouclé yarn; alpaca and cotton.

12.7 (above left) When plying hold the core yarn under tension, ply S with the wheel turning anticlockwise, and spiral the yarn around the core as in photo 12.5, but push the singles up at intervals to form the loops.

12.8 (below left) Plying knot yarn.

12.9 (below) Knot yarn.

KNOT YARN

Spin two singles, one dark and one light, with a Z twist (the wheel turns clockwise). Ply S (the wheel turning anticlockwise) holding the singles in separate hands and wind one single around the other in a figure 8 at intervals. For this sample I used one single of purple Corridale sliver and the other single was spun with tussah silk.

You can use two singles of the same colour for a textured but harmonious yarn. The knots are made with alternate singles to ensure that equal amounts will be used from each bobbin.

191

12.10 Tie the single to the leader with a knot. Then make another knot joining the leader and the single together about 12–15cm (5–6in) away from the first knot, making a loop your hand can fit through.

NAVAJO PLYING

This is a useful way to make a three-ply yarn from one bobbin. The singles yarn is chained in loops to form a triple yarn. Spin a singles Z twist (the wheel turns in a clockwise direction). Place the bobbin on a lazy kate. It doesn't take long before these actions become rhythmical. With practice, you can spin a multi-coloured single and make the chains so the colours in each chain are the same colour.

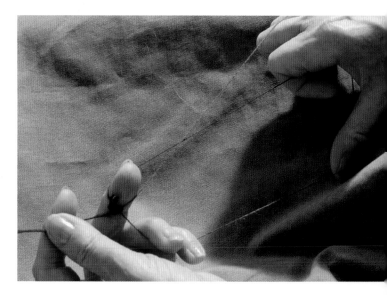

12.11 Put your back hand through this loop, grasping the single coming from the lazy kate, and pull it through to make another longer loop about 30cm (12in) long.

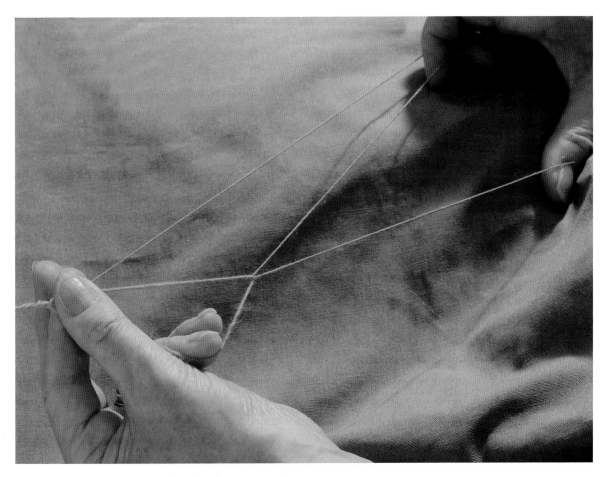

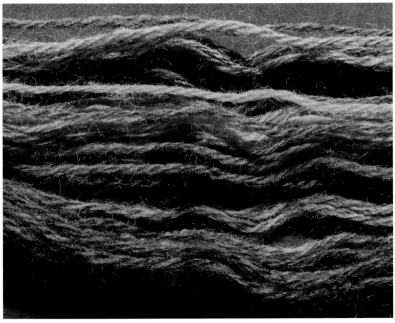

12.12 Begin treadling with the wheel turning in an anticlockwise direction (S twist) and let the twist run into the three strands, two of these strands are the loop yarn, and the third strand is the single. The front hand controls the twist while the back hand does the chaining. Treadle slowly to begin with until you have the hang of it.

12.13 Finished Navajo-plied yarn spun by Peter Sullivan.

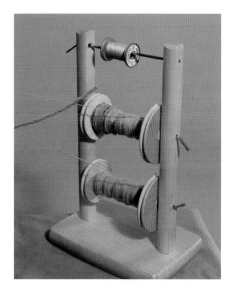

12.14 Place this spool onto the lazy kate with the two handspun singles, making sure the beads don't slip off in the process.

ADDING BEADS TO YARN

In photos 5.15a & b (pages 110 & 111), you can see how adding beads to a weft yarn while weaving adds glamour and a bit of glitz to your weaving. Now you can learn how to add beads while plying.

Spin two singles and place the two bobbins onto a lazy kate. It is a definite help if these bobbins are left overnight on the lazy kate to set as this stabilises the singles. You have enough to do when plying without having to untangle the singles because they are lively and twist around each other.

String the beads onto a fine strong thread in a colour that matches the handspun. In the sample I used a polyester sewing thread and added the beads onto the loose end while the polyester thread was still in its spool.

12.15 (above) Begin plying with the three threads. The two handspun singles and the polyester are joined firmly onto the leader. As you ply, slide a bead up the holding thread at intervals. The beads need to be small enough to go through the orifice and not catch on the hooks.

12.16 Beaded yarn.

FELTED YARN

Because the felting process strengthens the yarn, a single is all that is needed. I spun the green Corriedale sliver into a medium-weight yarn, with not much twist. Because Corriedale is half merino, it felts easily. I wound the single onto a niddy noddy and tied it in four places. When I took it off, it twisted up; however, the felting process will stabilise the yarn.

Put the skein into a bowl of hot, soapy water, swish it around a bit, then lay the skein onto a sheet of bubble wrap with the bubble side uppermost. This gives a roughened surface which helps the felting. Rub the skein up and down over the bubble wrap, adding more liquid soap as necessary. Test the felting process by pulling apart some of the strands. They should stick together a little but you should be able to separate them. Put the wet skein onto the swift (skeiner) or around a chair back if you don't have a swift and remove the ties. Then re-skein onto the niddy noddy, replace the ties, take the yarn off the niddy noddy, and repeat the washing and rubbing process. This felted yarn took me four repeats.

Rinse well and hang to dry. I did end up with lovely soft, clean hands as a bonus.

Felting tips

With some fibres, such as merino wool, which felts very easily, you can just rub the single yarn in your soapy hands, separating the strands now and then before they felt completely and then carrying on with the rubbing. This works for smaller skeins.

Novelty yarns make interesting felted yarn too, and all sorts of things can be added in the spinning process.

12.17 Felted yarn.

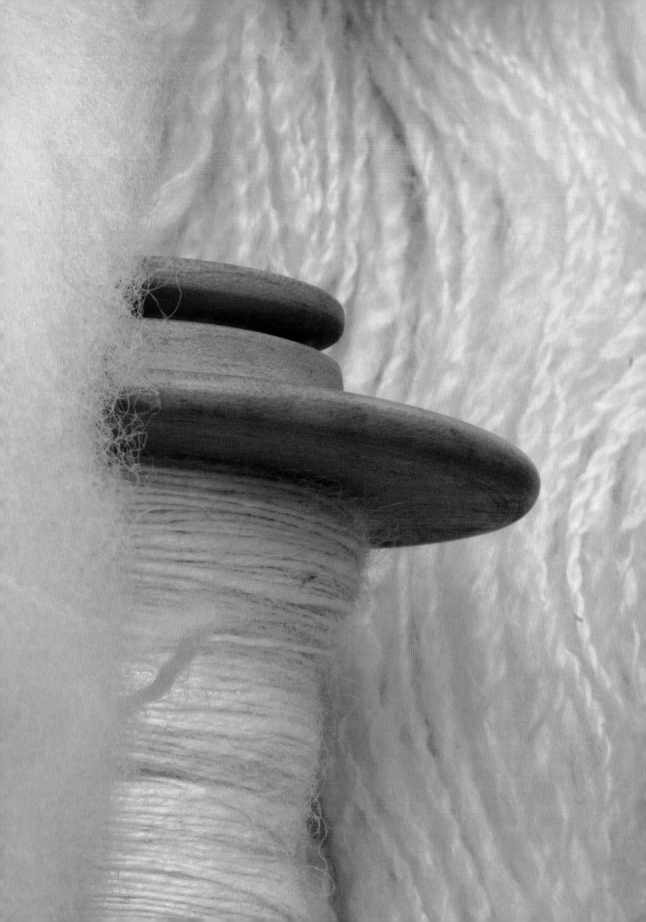

Glossary

Batt: mat of carded fibre.

Carding: process of opening fibres.

Charkha: the Indian word for a spinning wheel which is turned by hand.

Crimp: wave pattern in a fibre.

Drafting: pulling out and elongating the fibres before spinning.

Drive ratio: the difference between the drive wheel and bobbin or flyer whorl. This figure determines the amount of twist which will go into the yarn while spinning.

Fulling: also called milling. Meshing together of yarn when washed.

Great wheel: a spindle wheel. Also called a walking wheel.

Heddle: needle-like wire or string holders of warp yarn on a loom.

Lazy kate: bobbin holder.

Long draw: method of spinning woollen yarn.

Medium draft: method of spinning woollen yarn.

Micron: measures the diameter of a fibre: a millionth of a metre.

Niddy noddy: skeiner for making hanks of yarn.

Orifice: the hollowed-out end of the spindle shaft on a spinning wheel.

Pilling: tiny balls of fibre that form on a garment surface with wear.

Plying: twisting two or more yarns together.

Reed: metal comb-like device which separates and beats the weft on a loom.

Rolag: coil of woollen fibre.

Roving: long strand of carded or combed fibre.

Sett: spacing of warp threads on a loom.

Short backward draft: method of spinning worsted yarn.

Short forward draft: method of spinning worsted yarn.

Skein/skeiner: holder for putting yarn into hanks.

Single: one strand of yarn.

Skirting: removing dirty, matted or unsound fibres from a fleece before spinning.

Sliver: thinned out portion of the carded batt.

Spindle: a weighted shaft which turns to add twist to fibre.

Staple: bundle of fibres within a fleece. Also called a lock.

Tops: commercially prepared fibres that have been carded, then combed into a long, parallel formation with no twist.

Warp: the lengthwise threads on a loom.

Weft: the widthwise threads on a loom.

Woollen: yarn spun with the fibres randomly arranged. An airy, light yarn.

Worsted: yarn spun with parallel fibres of an even length.

Further reading

Arnot, Doe. *Spinning Camelid Fibre.* The New Zealand Spinning, Weaving and Woolcraft Society Inc., New Zealand, 2010.

Field, Anne. *Spinning Wool: Beyond the Basics.* David Bateman Ltd, Auckland, New Zealand, 2010.

Fournier, Nola & Jane. *In Sheep's Clothing.* Interweave Press, USA, 1995.

Garripoli, Amelia. *Productive Spindling.* Ask The Bellwether, www.thebellwether.com, USA, 2009.

Lowry, Priscilla. *The Secrets of Silk: From the Myths and Legends to the Middle Ages.* St John's Press, London, UK, 2003 (2nd ed. 2008.

MacKenzie McCuin, Judith. *The Intentional Spinner.* Interweave Press, USA, 2009.

Old, Pat. *In a Spin.* Sherborne Group, Tauranga, New Zealand, 2009.

Teal, Peter. *Hand Woolcombing and Spinning.* Robin & Russ Handweavers Inc., USA, 1993.

The Secrets of Silk: From Textiles to Fashion. St John's Press, London, UK, 2004.

Reeve, Jo. *The Ashford Book of Hand Spinning.* Ashford Handicrafts Ltd, Ashburton, New Zealand, 2009.

Varney, Diane. *Spinning Designer Yarns.* Interweave Press, USA, 1987.

Vester, Paula J. *Spinning Cotton.* World in a Spin Publishing, Georgia, USA, www.worldinaspin.com, 1996.

WEBSITES

www.treenwaysilks.com — Karen Selk's website has an excellent article on spinning silk by Celia Quinn.

www.nzsheep.co.nz — New Zealand Sheepbreeders Association website has comprehensive information on sheep breeds.

Index

alpaca 52, 56, 101–15
  changing the characteristics 108–9
  colour range 102
  cria 102, 103, 104
  crocheted hoodie 112–15
  plying 105, 107, 112
  projects 110–15
  shearing 102
  skirting 102
  uses 107–8
  washing fleece 102
  washing yarn 107
  woven beaded scarf 110–11
alpaca/cotton yarn 190–1
alpaca/silk yarn 175, 176
angora/merino yarn 186, 187
angora rabbit 141–7
  characteristics 142
  novelty yarn 145
  preparation 143
  projects 146–7
  spinning 143–5
  uses 145
animal fibres 82–147; see also alpaca; angora
  rabbit; mohair; silk; wool
Ashford wheels 17, 22, 47

baby wear 43, 107
bamboo 150, 167
batts 15; see also carding
beads, adding to yarn 111, 194
beanie, child's 186–7
bearings 45, 46
beret for child, crocheted cotton 161
black fleeces 87, 94, 101, 109
blankets 51, 57, 63, 69, 91, 93, 108, 135
blended fibres 175–87
  blending your own fibres 179–81
  brushing finished garment 182
  checking 176
  commercially prepared fibre 176–8
  plying 182

bobbin-led wheels 21, 38, 44, 48
  determining drive ratio 40
bobbin whorl 38, 39, 40
bobbins 18, 19, 20, 21, 22, 23–4
  problem solving 32, 49
bombyx silk 118, 121, 123, 127
booties 146
Borderdale breed 87
bottom-whorl spindle 69, 70
bouclé yarn 191
brake band 22, 23, 29, 39, 48
  problem solving 24, 32, 49
brake band tension knob 19, 49
breaks in wool 86, 96, 102

cardigan for teddy bear, cotton 162–3
carding
  commercially-prepared fleeces 15–16, 51
  cotton 154, 156
  problem solving 55, 60, 63
  see also combs and combing; drum-carding;
    hand-carding; flick-carding; mini-combs
carpets 129
cellulose fibres 165–7
charkha wheels 17, 18, 157
cleanliness of fleece 96; see also dirty fleeces;
  washing fleeces
clothing fabric 63, 69, 73–4, 92, 129
coat fabric 63, 73–4, 133
coats for sheep 94
coats, knitted 93
coloured fleeces 87, 94, 101, 109
combs and combing 16, 54–5, 57, 68, 94, 104,
  105, 106
  problem solving 55
commercially-prepared fibre 15–16, 51, 53–4,
  58–9, 64, 68
  alpaca 104, 105, 109
  blended 176–8
  cotton 156
  mohair 131
Coopworth breed 52, 87

core yarns 134–5, 169
Corriedale breed 88, 195
   characteristics of wool 91
   source of fleeces 99
   spinning 91
   uses 91
Corriedale/mohair yarn 178
cortex 86
cotton/alpaca yarn 190–1
cotton yarn 153–63
   characteristics 155
   commercially prepared fibre 156
   plying 159
   preparation 156
   problem solving 159, 160
   projects 161–3
   sample skeins 153
   spinning 155, 157–9
   uses 160
   washing 160
crankshaft 19
crimp 15, 95–6
   alpaca 102, 103, 105
crocheted hoodie 112–15
cuticle 86

dirty fleeces 53, 95, 97
diz 55, 132
Dorset Down breed 93
double-drive wheels 21, 39, 46, 48, 49
   adjusting tension 23–4
   bobbin and flyer whorls 38
   determining drive ratio 39
   spinning fine yarn 43
double-treadle wheels 21, 46
Down breeds
   characteristics of wool 93
   spinning 93
   uses 93
drafting 15, 16, 24–5
   problem solving 26
   silk 119
   see also long draw; medium draft; short
      backward draft; short forward draft
drive band 19, 22, 23, 24, 38, 39, 44, 48
   problem solving 24, 32, 49
   see also string cord drive band

drive band tension knob 19, 48, 49
drive ratio 19, 38–40, 44
   spinning cotton 157
   and twist count 40–1
drive wheels 19, 20, 24, 37, 46; *see also* single-
   drive wheels; double-drive wheels
drum-carding 16, 60, 62, 63, 64, 94, 109, 134
   blended fibres 179, 181
drying wool after washing 31, 97, 121
Drysdale breed 15, 87

Egyptian cotton 154
electronic spinning wheels 45
Elizabeth wheel 23–4, 46
embroidery yarn 57, 121
   cross-stitch project 72
English angora 142
English Leicester (Leicester Longwool) breed
   31, 52, 87, 91
   characteristics of wool 93
   spinning 93
   uses 93

felting
   avoiding, when washing fleece and yarn 32,
      89, 97
   method for felting yarn 195
   shrink-proofing 88
   singles 28
fibre, spinning
   joining on new supply 27
   see also spinning process
fibres, *see* animal fibres; blended fibres;
   manufactured fibres; plant fibres
fine wool and yarn 42, 88, 89, 90, 150
   spinning 42–3, 45
flax 52
fleeces, wool 85–6
   black and coloured 94
   choosing, for spinning 82, 96
   commercially prepared 15–16
   dirty 53, 95, 97
   preparation 52–3
   removing staples 98
   samples from different breeds 87
   storing 96, 97
   unwashed 16, 53

see also skirting fleeces; staples; washing fleeces; wool
flick-carding 56, 68, 94, 104, 105, 106, 132
flyer-led wheels 19, 21, 38, 157
   determining drive ratio 39
flyer whorl 37, 38
flyers 19, 21, 22, 23–4, 38, 39
   problem solving 32
   see also jumbo flyer; lace flyer and bobbin
folding wheels 20
footman 19, 39
frame loom, 20cm (8in) 138
French angora 142

German angora 142
gloves 44, 69, 91, 92, 107
Gotland breed 87
Gotland/silk yarn 184, 185
grease 15, 32, 53, 86, 96, 97
great wheels 17, 18, 157
grooves, drive-wheel 39

hairy wool 86, 95
Hampshire Down 93
   half-bred 87
hand-carding 16, 60–1, 64, 94, 109, 134
   blended fibres 179, 180
hats 44, 63, 66, 69, 75, 91, 92, 107, 135, 160, 175
high-whorl (top-whorl) spindle 69, 70
hoodie, crocheted 112–15
hooks 27, 44, 49, 69
horizontal (Saxony) wheels 20, 46
huacaya alpaca 101, 103, 108
   characteristics 103
   commercially prepared fibre 104
   preparation 104
   spinning 103, 104
   worsted spinning 104–5

Irish tension 23, 48, 49

jackets 57, 63, 73, 92, 93, 133
   crocheted hoodie 112–15
   spun and knitted in Romney wool 98–9
jerseys 44, 51, 57, 63, 68, 91, 93, 107, 135, 160
jumbo flyer 44

knitting yarn 42, 57, 63, 66, 68–9, 75, 90, 92, 93, 98
   alpaca 107, 109
   angora 145
   cotton 160
   mohair 132, 135
   silk 121, 123, 124
knot yarn 191

lace flyer and bobbin 43
lazy kate 20, 28
leader 22, 24–5
Lincoln breed 52, 87, 90, 91
lock, *see* staple
long draw 64, 66–7, 68, 159
Lyocell (Tencel) 150, 165, 166

maidens 19, 23, 24, 32
manufactured fibres 150, 165–9
mawata silk caps and handkerchiefs 122–3, 127
measuring amount of yarn needed for projects 32, 74
medium draw 64, 65, 68, 159
medium yarn 15, 42, 51
   spinning 44
mercerized cotton 154
merino 31, 72, 76, 79, 86, 87, 88
   blended with angora 143, 144–5
   characteristics 89
   grease 89, 97
   project 76–9
   spinning 89
   uses 89
   washing fleeces 89
merino angora yarn 186, 187
merino/possum yarn 177–8
merino/silk yarn 178, 183
merino/Tencel yarn 182
microns 88
   alpaca 103
   see also names of sheep breeds, e.g., Romney breed
mini-combs 54–5, 68, 104, 132
   blended fibres 179
mittens 44, 63, 91, 107, 135, 160
mohair 52, 54, 129–39

changing the characteristics 133–5
characteristics 130
commercially prepared fibre 131, 133
preparation 132, 134
projects 136–9
skirting the fleece 130
spinning 131, 132, 134–5
uses 129, 132–3
mohair/Corriedale yarn 178
moorit fleeces 94
mother-of-all 22, 23, 24, 42–3, 49

niddy noddy 20, 30
noils 58, 68
mohair 134
silk 119, 121, 122, 123
novelty yarns 135, 172, 182, 189–95
angora 145
nylon 169
nylon brake band 39
nylon drive band 23

oil points 45, 46
Optim™ 88
orifice 22, 24, 25, 44, 46, 49
organically grown cotton 154
outdoor garments 15, 51, 57, 63, 88, 92,
93, 107, 133

Perendale breed 87
pigmentation, *see* black fleeces; coloured
fleeces
pilling 53, 89, 94
Pima cotton 154
plant fibres 150–63
plying, and plied yarns
alpaca 105, 107, 112
cotton 159
Navajo plying 192–3
semi-worsted yarn 63
silk 120
spindle spinning 71
testing for twist 29
textured yarns 190, 191, 192–3
two different yarns 182
three-ply yarn 191, 192–3
twist count, spinning and plying 31, 32, 41

washing plied yarn and setting the twist
31–2, 107
woollen yarn 27–9, 64
worsted yarn 57, 107
Polwarth breed 87, 90
characteristics of wool 90
Romney/Polwarth cross breed 58–9
source of fleeces 99
spinning 90
uses 90
Polwarth/silk yarn 180
pom-poms 176–7
possum/merino yarn 177–8
pre-drafting 54–5, 119
puni 156, 157, 159

rayon 165
rolag 58, 59, 62, 65
Romney breed 15, 52, 53, 79, 87, 88
characteristics of wool 92
projects 73–4, 75, 98–9
sources of fleeces 99
spinning 92
uses 92
Romney/Polwarth cross breed 58–9
rovings 15–16, 53, 54, 68
alpaca 104, 105
rugs 15, 57, 63, 93
runner 34–5

S twist 31, 112, 190, 191
Saxony (horizontal) wheels 20, 46
scales
alpaca 101, 105
wool 15, 86
scarves 43, 89, 90, 91
scarves, knitted 33, 66, 76–9, 109, 123, 135,
145, 160
merino/silk 183
silk 125
scarves, woven 66, 109, 121, 135, 145
angora 146–7
beaded alpaca 110–11
mohair 137
silk 126–7
Scotch tension 17, 22, 24, 48, 49
Sea Island cotton 154

SeaCell 166
second-hand wheels 20
semi-woollen spinning 68
   alpaca 109
   blended fibre 179
   mohair 133
semi-woollen yarn
   characteristics 68
   commercially prepared fibre 68
   preparation 68
   problem solving 68
   uses 68–9
semi-worsted spinning 58, 63
   alpaca 109
   alpaca/silk fibre 176
   blended fibre 179
   mohair 133, 135
semi-worsted yarn
   commercially prepared fibre 58–9
   plying 63
   preparation 60–2
   problem solving 58, 63
   uses 63
shawls 15, 43, 66, 89, 90, 91, 108, 109, 123, 132, 135, 145
   feather & fan knitted shawl/scarf 76–9
   spinning wheel shawl 184–5
short backward draft 25, 26–7, 157
short forward draft 24–5, 157, 176
shrinkage 31, 32, 35, 82, 130, 166, 168, 172, 182
shrink-proofing wool 88
Shropshire breed 93
silk/alpaca yarn 175, 176
silk caps and handkerchiefs 122–3, 127
silk/Gotland yarn 184, 185
silk/merino yarn 178, 183
silk/Polwarth yarn 180
silk yarn 52, 117–27
   changing the characteristics 121–4
   characteristics 118
   plying 120
   problem solving 121
   projects 125–6
   spinning 118–20, 122
   uses 121
   washing 120–1

single-drive flyer-led wheel (Scotch tension) 17, 22, 24, 48, 49
single-treadle wheels 21, 46
singles 27–8
   felting 28
skeining 30–1
   spindle spinning 71
skirt fabric 73, 92, 133
skirting fleeces 95–6
   alpaca 102
   mohair 130
sliver 15, 58–9, 64; *see also* carding
socks 63, 69, 92, 93, 132
   knitted socks project 136
Southdown breed 93
soy fibre 168
spindle shaft 18
spindle spinning 69–71
   embroidered cross-stitch project 72
   plying 71
   skeining 71
spindle whorl 17, 19, 69
spindles 17, 18, 69, 70
spinning process and methods 24–7
   alpaca 103, 104–7
   angora 143–5
   core yarn, spinning around 134–5
   cotton 157–9
   mohair 131, 132, 134–5
   problem solving 26, 32
   silk 116–18
   spindle spinning 69–71, 72
   spinning from the fold 69
   textured yarn 180, 190, 191
   see also semi-woollen spinning; semi-worsted spinning; woollen spinning; worsted spinning
spinning wheels 17–19
   different drive ratios 41
   maintenance 45
   problem solving 49
   second-hand 20
   types 46–9
   types for beginners 19–20
spiral yarn 190–1
staples 15, 16, 52, 54
   alpaca 102

breaks in 96, 102
broken and weak tips 89, 94, 96, 102
mohair 132, 134
removing from fleece 96
see also crimp
static electricity 86, 109, 155, 169
storing fleeces 96, 97, 102
string cord drive band 42–3
Suffolk breed 93
suri alpaca 101
characteristics 105
commercially prepared fibre 105
preparation 106
spinning 105–6
worsted spinning 106–7
sweaters 44
synthetic fibres 169

techniques, basic 21–4
teddy bear cotton cardigan 162–3
Tencel (Lyocell) 150, 165, 166
Tencel/merino yarn 182
tension 21–2, 26, 32, 49, 68; *see also* Irish
tension; Scotch tension
Texel breed 87
textured yarn 34, 35, 72, 121, 122, 123, 135,
182, 189
thick wool and yarn 42, 150
spinning 44, 45
threading hook 22
three-ply yarn 191, 192–3
throws 51, 108, 135
mohair, project 138–9
throwsters silk 124, 127
top-whorl (high-whorl) spindle 69, 70
tops 15–16, 53, 54, 68
alpaca 104, 105
cotton 154
silk 118, 119
treadles 17, 19, 21
treadling 21, 24, 32
tussah silk 118, 121, 123, 125
twists (per 2.5cm)
alpaca 105
in drafting area 26, 57
drive ratio and twist count 40–1
regulating 40–1

spinning and plying twist and size 31, 32, 41
testing for correct amount 29
washing plied yarn and setting the
twist 31–2
see also drive ratio; S twist; Z twist

upholstery fabric 93, 129, 133
upright (vertical) wheels 20, 46, 47

vertical (upright) wheels 20, 46, 47

washed yarn
alpaca 107
dirty yarn 32, 53
leaving grease in 32, 53
silk 120–1
washing plied yarn, and setting the twist
31–2, 107
washing fleeces 15, 89, 96–7
alpaca 102
merino 89
mohair 131
weaving yarn 42, 57, 63, 66, 69, 92
alpaca 108, 109
angora 145
cotton 160
mohair 133, 135
silk 121, 123, 124
whorls 17, 23, 41; *see also* bobbin whorl; flyer
whorl; spindle whorl
wool 82, 85–6
characteristics 86
commercially-prepared 15–16, 51, 53–4,
58–9, 64, 68
enhancement of qualities 88
hairy 86, 95
preparation 54–7
structure 86
see also fleeces; and names of breeds,
e.g., merino
wool combs 54
Woolee Winder 27
woollen spinning 64–7
alpaca 108, 109
angora 143–4
blended fibres 178, 179
mohair 133, 134–5

silk 123, 124
woollen yarn
    characteristics 64
    commercially prepared fibre 64, 109
    differences from worsted spun yarn 51
    plying 27–9, 64
    problem solving 64, 67
    project 98–9
    uses 66, 109
    washing 96–7
    see also semi-woollen yarn
worsted spinning 52–57
    alpaca 104–5, 106–7, 108
    mohair 131, 132
    silk 119–20, 122, 123, 124
worsted yarn
    commercially prepared fibre 53–4, 104, 105,
        131–2
    differences from woollen spun yarn 51
    preparation 54–7, 96, 106
    plying 57, 107
    uses 57
    woven fabric project 73–4
    see also semi-worsted yarn
wrapped spiral yarn 190
wraps (per 2.5cm) 41, 42

yarns
    breaking 26
    calculating amount needed for
        projects 32, 74
    measuring size 41–4
    problem solving 32
    see also fine wool and yarn; knitting yarn;
        medium yarn; semi-worsted yarn; thick
        wool and yarn; weaving yarn; woollen
        yarn; worsted yarn

Z twist 31, 112, 144, 190, 191